NOT JUST A LIVING

*The Complete Guide to Creating a
Business That Gives You a Life*

MARK HENRICKS

PERSEUS
PUBLISHING
A Member of the Perseus Books Group

Library of Congress Control Number: 2002105972
ISBN 0-7382-0812-4

Perseus Publishing is a member of the Perseus Books Group.

Find us on the World Wide Web at http://www.perseuspublishing.com

Perseus Publishing books are available at special discounts for bulk purchases in the U.S. by corporations, institutions, and other organizations. For more information, please contact the Special Markets Department at the Perseus Books Group, 11 Cambridge Center, Cambridge, MA 02142, or call (617) 252–5298, (800) 255-1514, or email j.mccrary@perseusbooks.com.

Text design by Jeffrey Williams
Set in 11-point Apollo MT by Perseus Books Group

First paperback printing, June 2003

2 3 4 5 6 7 8 9 10—05 04 03

NOT JUST A LIVING

Also by Mark Henricks

Grow Your Business
Mastering Home Networking
Business Plans Made Easy

This book is for Barbara

Contents

Acknowledgments

Thanks first to the hundreds of lifestyle entrepreneurs who shared their stories. Special recognition goes to Mark Abouzeid, Hugh Daniels, Maryalice Hurst, Dave Jacobs, Ron Kipp, Robin Knepp, Cheryl Leonhardt, Joyce Meskis, Michelle Paster, Jane Pollak, and Brad Stillahn. Their particular candor and consideration, along with their remarkable experiences as lifestyle entrepreneurs, helped this book enormously.

Alison Hubbard, formerly of The Professional Association of Innkeepers International, agreeably passed my request for information on to the association's entire membership, many of whom responded with useful accounts of their pursuit of lifestyle entrepreneurship. Lesley Spencer of Home-Based Working Moms similarly helped out by broadcasting my appeal to her organization's members, a number of whom contributed stories that appear here.

Nancy Stevens and Lori Stacy understood and appreciated the idea of lifestyle entrepreneurship before almost anyone and were in a position to provide important editorial support that allowed me to complete the early research to prove the concept. Some key interviews were initiated and parts of the first chapter were written to fulfill an assignment to write an article for *American Way* magazine, where they worked at the time. My editors at *Entrepreneur* magazine, including Peggy Bennett, Karen Axelton, and Janean Chun, have given me endless guidance and many paying assignments during the last dozen years of researching and writing articles on entrepreneurship.

Karl Vesper is probably the author whose writing on entrepreneurs I refer to most often, here and elsewhere. His books provide the answer to almost any question about entrepreneurs. Jay Conrad Levinson and Seth Godin have, over the years, provided inspiration and opportunities that encouraged me to pursue my own particular brand of lifestyle entrepreneurship as a business author. Thanks to Robert Reich for writing *The Future of Success* (Knopf, 2001). I was reading his book about how our ideas of success are changing when the idea for *Not Just a Living* first appeared.

A lot of authors thank agents. James Levine of James Levine Communications deserves more than that. I hope he will be pleased nonetheless to receive this praise for his unusual blend of editorial expertise, marketing skill, and never-failing pleasant manner. Among the hundreds of editors I have worked with, Nick Philipson, executive editor at Perseus Publishing, is exceptional for his enthusiasm, his patience, and his kind and accurate criticisms. I am indebted to Lynn Goldberg and Camille McDuffie of Goldberg McDuffie Communications for offering their critical, timely support for this project.

Finally I wish to thank my wife, Barbara Cave Henricks, who does everything perfectly and in less time than seems possible, and our children, Kate, Corey, and Brady, who stamp our lives with their own special styles every day.

Austin, Texas
April 2002

Introduction

Maybe it didn't rank with the Bill of Rights and the Magna Carta as far as its impact on humanity, but the document I pulled out of my typewriter in November 1986 seemed to me to be my own personal Declaration of Independence. It was a letter addressed to the local publisher of the newspaper company I had been working for as a reporter and editor for the last five years. "I am writing to inform you of my decision to resign my position to pursue a freelance writing career," it said. It thanked my employers for the opportunity to work there and told them that my decision was effective in two weeks.

The letter was courteous, cool, and professional. The terse prose radiated assurance, commitment, and confidence. It would be hard for them to argue with, although I was sure they'd try. I imagined them making me offers I couldn't refuse and saw myself rejecting their promotions and raises, smiling indulgently because they simply didn't get it. That was understandable, because it wasn't exactly in the letter. But the fact was, I didn't want more money. I didn't want a promotion—especially if it came on my employer's terms, which would certainly include relocating to another city.

What I was after, in my move to become a self-employed journalist, was a lifestyle. That letter announced not just a resignation, but the blossoming into reality of an existence that I had dreamed of since college and had been working at part-time for almost as long as I'd been a reporter.

Some of my motivation came from the desire to rid my life of things I didn't want to be there. I didn't want to commute across the breadth of Dallas County at rush hour anymore. I didn't care to be constrained to reporting on company earnings, annual meetings, and other local business events. I didn't want to be told that my annual raise, like everyone else's, would be limited to 3 percent this year because of problems elsewhere in the corporate empire of which we were a small part.

I wanted to write for more high-profile and more varied publications than the *Dallas-Fort Worth Business Journal*. I wanted to report on sports, health, and culture. I wanted to work from the home office I had put together from secondhand furniture in the dining room of the home I had recently bought. I wanted my earnings to reflect my abilities and efforts, not somebody else's unfortunate judgment.

I wanted this badly.

And that letter sat on my desk at home for six months, undelivered.

I looked at it from time to time, savoring the words, but watched forlornly as the date at the top receded ever further into the past. The letter would have to be rewritten to be handed in now, if it ever was.

But there were things that had to happen before I could become self-employed, and none of them were happening. Some seemed beyond my control. For instance, I needed to refinance my mortgage before giving up my steady paycheck, and I'd already been turned down for a loan. Others, such as some surgery I needed to undergo before separating from my company health insurance policy, were simply hard to face. Finally, I still wasn't sure you could actually make a living as a freelance writer, so the lifestyle, while appealing, seemed like little more than a dream.

One day, in a bitter mood, I crumpled the letter, tossed it away, and, instead of resigning from my job, resigned myself to the fact that my life was never going to change.

If you read the jacket of this book, or if you can read between the lines, you know that I overcame my despondency, surmounted the obstacles, updated and delivered that letter, and left my job to start an existence as an independent freelance writer. That lifestyle is now in its fifteenth year, and it has been a remarkably successful endeavor. I've completed well over a thousand assignments and never been without a backlog. I've seen my work published on topics from sports to personal finance in a number of America's largest and most prestigious publications.

Even more striking was the effect on my lifestyle. I've worked as many or as few hours as I deemed necessary. I attend virtually no meetings. My commute is measured in feet, not miles. I wear a tie so rarely that when I do, it often takes several tries to get the knot right. I've gotten paid for indulging my love of reading, as a book reviewer. I've been sent on fabulous travel adventures, all expenses paid. I receive, gratis, piles of high-tech gadgets from companies that want me to consider their products in articles and books about technology trends.

And I get paid to do all this. My lifestyle is part of, and is funded entirely by, my earnings as a lifestyle entrepreneur. I am not and never have been independently wealthy. I was born in the hills of Kentucky, and my first home was a trailer on the Army base at Fort Knox. I grew up the second of four children in the middle-class suburb of Irving, Texas. I attended public schools there and graduated, after a couple of false starts, from the journalism program of the University of Texas at Austin, perennially the nation's most populous campus and, therefore, arguably something of a diploma mill. The last job I quit, as assistant editor of the 20,000-circulation *Dallas-Fort Worth Business Journal*, paid $27,700 a year. That was better than the $9,800 salary earned at my first reporting job, covering the police beat for the *Beaumont Journal*, a now-defunct evening newspaper located in the swamps of southeast Texas. I am not in line for any inheritance that I know of, although if there are any long-lost relatives out there anxious to benefit me, let them come forth.

Fortunately, being a lifestyle business owner is more than a lifestyle. It's also a way to make a living. For doing all these things I'd like to do anyway, I am paid, plus expenses. It's enabled me to keep that first home while moving to New York City and then Austin. Along with my wife's earnings as a book publicist, it's paid for private nannies and put my children in private school. Though I work more to suit my lifestyle than my pocketbook and rarely put in over forty hours a week, I earn twice as much as a comparable magazine staff writer.

I never really expected to do this well financially. The main thing that attracted me to freelancing was the mystique of the freelance lifestyle. Freelance writing is considered a desirable occupation by many people. Much of this appeal, it turns out, is based on mistaken perceptions, including the idea that freelancers get paid for writing whatever they feel like writing about. But the point is that a lot of people are curious about freelance writing, and I've wound up advising and mentoring many of them as they attempted to make their own lifestyle employment dreams come true. I've helped them deal with doubt, develop their skills, identify their markets, and get their businesses off the ground.

It helps that my specialty for most of my journalism career has been business—specifically, small business. I've written a small business management column since 1992 for *Entrepreneur* magazine, and my reporting on trends and techniques of starting and running a small business has appeared in many other small business publications. I have interviewed thousands of entrepreneurs and small business advisors for articles and books about why and how businesses are begun and run.

One of the unfortunate things about being a journalist is having to write about things of which you have no firsthand experience. Like a couch-potato sportswriter covering Olympic athletics, I have often found myself trying to get inside the heads of people I share little background with and describe activities in which I have never engaged. At times, this can be agreeably challenging. It is more often unsettling, because you fear being found out as a fraud. From time to time, I had wondered what it would be like to write about a topic that I really knew because I had lived it. That's one of the reasons I have been so active in mentoring other freelance writers. I don't have to quote experts on that topic; I am an expert. I find this comforting.

All of these experiences have combined to make the conception, research, and writing of *Not Just a Living* a joyful experience for me.

To explain: Many, many of the entrepreneurs I have spoken with have told me of motivations for founding their businesses that had nothing to do with the conventional conception of an entrepreneur's goal—namely, to get rich quick. Some, to be sure, were clearly interested only in a rapid return on as small an investment as possible, to be followed by retirement to a chateau on Lake Austin. The late 1990s were inhabited by a dense population of this type, but they are familiar to me as well from the early 1980s oil boom in Houston as well as the Dallas real-estate lending scandals of the late 1980s.

But when I stopped to think about what kind of book would be the most useful to write, for today and for today's people and their problems, it seemed clear that a book about starting a business that would address lifestyle issues more than business issues could be useful. At the least, it would allow me to take my experience as a lifestyle entrepreneur and join it with my grasp of the entrepreneur's challenges gained through much observation and commentary. This book, with the help of literary agent James Levine and Perseus Books editor Nick Philipson, is the result.

Not Just a Living is not just another start-a-business manual. I've written those, and I know the difference. Most deal in a page or a paragraph with lifestyle motivations for starting a business. Some others, notably the work-at-home genre and the hymns to going solo, are more focused on lifestyle, but they still don't address the full scope and power of a business's potential to affect your lifestyle. Being a lifestyle entrepreneur is more than staying home with the kids, although it can be that. It can also be staying home with an ailing spouse, aging parents, or simply yourself. It's more than being your own boss and more than going solo, although it most emphatically is about taking responsibility for managing yourself.

Being a lifestyle entrepreneur is about getting off the constant travel grind and deciding when and where you want to go instead of being subject to the whims of a macho, masochistic road warrior corporate culture. It's about living where you want, whether that's New York City or a mountaintop in Montana, instead of moving your family—like it or not—when you're transferred to a new office every few years.

It's about working with the people you like and not being stuck with bossy bosses, hopelessly demanding customers, and backstabbing so-called colleagues. It's about doing the work you want, whether that's skippering a charter sailboat, teaching kids to read, or working with environmentally responsible organizations.

Being a lifestyle entrepreneur is not about being in business so much as it is about being you. That may sound merely pseudo-profound, but I think that if you take the plunge I'm about to describe and then look back on that statement after a few years, you'll agree that it truly is a meaningful concept. That's why the first part of this book deals with addressing the question of whether you are, in fact, a potential lifestyle entrepreneur and, if so, what kind of lifestyle entrepreneur you might be (Chapters 1 and 2). As part of that—in a chapter that my training as an objective reporter requires of me—I detail the potential downside of being a lifestyle entrepreneur (Chapter 3). The first part concludes with a look at the challenge of actually making the decision to cut the cor-porate strings and become a lifestyle entrepreneur, as well as myriad ways to make the break (Chapter 4).

In Part 2, you will be exposed to the practical realities of lifestyle entrepreneurialism. You'll learn about your basic options for becoming a lifestyle entrepreneur (Chapter 5), including starting a new enter-prise, buying an existing concern, franchising, and freelancing. Next, you'll see what it takes to design a business that actually generates money—a requirement if your enterprise is to financially support your lifestyle (Chapter 6). Then you'll survey the options for raising the start-up funds it will take to get your business under way (Chapter 7).

The third part deals with four key concerns of lifestyle entrepre-neurs: selecting the people they will work with and for, choosing and managing technology, achieving the proper mix of growth and con-trol, and cashing out at the end. People hassles from officious bosses, combative colleagues, impossible customers, and unfeeling bureau-crats collectively compose one of the most powerful impetuses toward entrepreneurship for many lifestyle seekers. Why suffer them after you've made your break? So the first chapter in this section (Chapter 8) shows how and why you should exercise your lifestyle entrepreneur right to associate with the particular employees, customers, suppliers, and others who will have the strongest possible positive effect on your lifestyle.

Chapter 9 is dear to my heart: technology. Gadgets like cell phones, laptops, and personal digital assistants can make it possible for entrepreneurs to have the lifestyle they want—or they can make it impossible. This chapter will show how to assess your technology needs and stay on top of your technology and keep it from ruling over you. Chapter 10 deals with two of the most pernicious myths of entrepreneurship, namely, that every enterprise must pursue growth in order to survive and that you can't grow without grief. You'll learn that you can choose to grow or not to grow without sacrificing either the benefits of your lifestyle or the viability of your business. The concluding chapter explodes another of the pervasive myths about entrepreneurs who are mainly in it for the lifestyle. That is, that they won't get any or as many of the lasting financial rewards accruing to those who are in it strictly for the money. The dictum to "do what you love, the money will follow" is, unfortunately, unrealistic. It's more complicated than that. But if you arrange things carefully, you can create a lifestyle business that will build wealth adequate to supply both your short-term and long-term needs. You can create an enterprise of lasting value—to pay for a child's college, to fund your own retirement, or even to bequeath to your heirs. It can be an asset to be liquidated or a venture through which future generations can express their own lifestyles. The appendix offers a list of additional resources.

A lot of this story is my story. The pal who encouraged me to try just one more time to refinance my mortgage is a common theme among the lifestyle entrepreneurs who reported a spouse, partner, or friend provided emotional support just when it was needed. My experience of moonlighting in my chosen field of entrepreneurship while remaining employed full-time turned out to be one of the most common paths others took to test the waters of lifestyle business ownership. Avoiding overly demanding customers, negotiating firmly but respectfully for fair prices for my services, and being willing to take what seem like foolish fliers (such as moving to New York City with no job, no savings, no apartment, and not a single friend in the city) because I was sure I could make it or, at the very least, could survive failure—these turn out to be the experiences of many other lifestyle entrepreneurs as well.

I will close this introduction with some good news. The introduction has been my story, and I'll come back to my personal experiences where appropriate through this book, but it would be antithetical to the concept of the lifestyle entrepreneur to try to express it through a single example. This book is about more than me. You are about to meet more lifestyle entrepreneurs of more varieties and with more unique modes of expression than you probably ever imagined existed. Each comes with a lesson to be learned or an inspiration to be grasped. I hope you enjoy meeting them and are moved to join us.

PART ONE

Are You a Lifestyle Entrepreneur?

ONE

Imagining the Ideal Life

R on Kipp's colleagues thought he was crazy. He was making excellent money, with prospects for a long career at one of the world's top companies. Yet he was quitting his $100,000-a-year job at IBM to move to the Cayman Islands to become an entrepreneur. And not just any entrepreneur—the owner of a scuba diving tour company.

"A giant stride into madness," Ron says. "That's what people said I was doing when I left IBM to go into diving." The year was 1981, when $100,000 was worth approximately $200,000 in today's dollars. So it's not hard to understand why Ron's sanity became suspect among his soon-to-be ex-officemates. And they wouldn't have been reassured by much of what took place next.

The first few years, Ron paid himself an annual salary of $12,000— about what IBM paid him every six weeks. Instead of a $180,000 house in a comfortable Cleveland suburb, he slept in a converted harborside warehouse with no stove or bathroom. Rather than overseeing a white-collar workforce, he *was* the workforce, filling air tanks, guiding tours, and sweeping floors for long hours daily.

Despite all this, the possibility of clambering back into his dark suit and wing tips rarely, if ever, crossed his mind. "I loved it," Ron says. "I looked at the boats outside, and they were mine. When I swept the floors, they were mine." When winter snow covered Ohio, Ron basked in tropical balm. When his ex-colleagues were trapped in endless meetings, Ron floated free in crystalline Caribbean water on one of his more than 5,500 scuba dives.

Twenty years later, Ron is still doing it. "I'm never going to retire," he declared over coffee one Sunday morning at his residence in the Cayman's capital city of George Town. "How could I? Ninety-nine percent of the poor slobs in the world wish they could do this."

Indeed they do. Today the term most likely to be applied to Ron is not "crazy," it's "lifestyle entrepreneur." A lifestyle entrepreneur is somebody who goes into business not primarily for financial rewards, but for lifestyle reasons. The lifestyle payoff may be living on the beach, in the mountains, or near a resort. It may be working fewer or more flexible hours, staying home to care for young children or aging parents, escaping the tyranny of corporate supervision, doing the kind of work you love, or any combination of the above. Lifestyle entrepreneurs don't want to be the next Bill Gates so much as the next Ron Kipp.

And they're anything but rare. As many as 90 percent of the roughly 20 million American small business owners appear to be motivated by lifestyle more than money, according to John Warrillow, president of a Toronto market research company specializing in the small business market. Studies on motivation by Warrillow & Co. identify three types of small business owners. "Mountain Climbers" are driven to increase sales and achieve business success. That's the traditional concept of the entrepreneur, John notes, yet these go-getters represent just 10 percent of small business owners. Thirty percent are "Freedom Fighters" seeking mainly independence and the opportunity to call their own shots and work when they want, where they want, and for whom they want. The rest, 60 percent, are "Craftspeople" motivated by the desire to do a particular type of work and do it well. "Craftspeople don't even think of themselves as entrepreneurs," John says. "They think of themselves as plumbers, photographers, or whatever."[1]

All of these people are, unquestionably, in business, and other studies support Warrillow's findings of their lifestyle motivations. A 1999 Lou Harris survey, cited by author Dan Pink in his paean to self-employment, *Free Agent Nation* (Warner, 2001), found money was the main driver for very few small entrepreneurs and self-employed people. Fully nine of ten said a desire for independence prompted them to become entrepreneurs.

Lifestyle entrepreneurship isn't getting any rarer either. "It's a trend," says Don Bradley, executive director of the Small Business Advancement National Center at the University of Central Arkansas. "I'm seeing it more and more." Don says lifestyle entrepreneurs who come to him for help striking out on their own tend to be burned-out mid-careerists. Many are corporate executives, while some are refugees from dot-com start-ups that went bust. Instead of working a hundred hours a week trying to surf the next new thing to an IPO, they're starting distinctly more laid-back businesses—restoring log cabins, building one-of-a-kind furniture, and running Ozark bed-and-breakfasts.

Part of the push into lifestyle entrepreneurialism stems from the fact that in the early years of the new millennium, the global economy has been taking a breather. Jobs haven't always been as plentiful as they were during the bull-market 1990s. "As the economy tanks, the percentage of Craftspeople increases," John Warrillow explains. "There's a very strong correlation."

Lifestyle entrepreneurship can be a comfortable refuge in rocky times. Just ask Ron Kipp. Today Bob Soto's Diving Ltd., the nearly moribund outfit Ron took over twenty years ago, is one of the biggest businesses in Grand Cayman, with seven boats, five locations, and forty-five employees. Ron is now a bona fide millionaire entrepreneur, but he's already been living the lifestyle many would-be millionaires dream of for the last two decades. "It all worked out," Ron says, looking back on his giant stride into lifestyle entrepreneurship. "It wasn't just a lark."

Drawing the Lifestyle Line

In a sense, all entrepreneurs are lifestyle entrepreneurs. Running a business is, if anything, more consuming than working at a job. That makes it all but impossible to separate entrepreneurship from lifestyle.

The essential difference is the degree of focus on money, on sales growth, and on expansion for expansion's sake.

Another key difference is that lifestyle ventures generally are not run for the financial benefit of someone else, such as investors who backed the enterprise in hopes of achieving a rich return. The first use of the term "lifestyle entrepreneur," as far as I can tell, was by University of New Hampshire professor William Wetzel in a 1987 magazine article.[2] Professor Wetzel, an expert on venture capital, was specifically using the term to refer to businesses that, because they are not being run primarily in pursuit of financial gain, can't expect to be financed by the usual sources. "There's no interest in a venture like that on the part of an outside investor, because it will never be sold for a capital gain," the professor explains. "In financial jargon, they have no upside potential for creating wealth. They may provide a handsome income for the small businessperson, but there's no potential for wealth creation."

Now might be a good time to point out that this book is also not about the likes of Martha Stewart. She has been described as a lifestyle entrepreneur because her business empire, Martha Stewart Living Omnimedia Inc., is all about disseminating information on cooking, decorating, gardening, and other activities considered part of a lifestyle. Martha's business certainly is closely related to her lifestyle. But it is also a publicly held, New York Stock Exchange–listed corporation with $286 million in annual revenues, 585 employees, and a compound annual sales growth rate for the four years ending in 2000 of 29 percent.[3] That is far enough removed from the central idea of a lifestyle entrepreneur that we can exclude her as an example.

Don't get me wrong—I haven't run across a single lifestyle entrepreneur who isn't interested in making a living and maybe a lot more from his or her business. Some of them are doing far better than getting by and, in fact, are quite successful by any standard. Lifestyle entrepreneurs aren't hobbyists. They're businesspeople, and their enterprises are intended to make money. For the purposes of this book, however, entrepreneurs who are doing it primarily to get rich aren't lifestyle entrepreneurs. Those who are doing it to rule a commercial empire aren't doing it for lifestyle. But even ruling out those commonly ascribed motivations, there are still plenty of other motivations for lifestyle entrepreneurs.

Making Your Own Decisions

A fierce desire for independence is probably the most common lifestyle motivation of any lifestyle entrepreneur. This is true whether you're talking about Americans, with their insistence on individualism, or lifestyle entrepreneurs from other cultures. In the United Kingdom, for example, a poll of start-up businesses found that only 12 percent of the founders considered money the main reason for their ventures. About a third of them were in search of a change of direction. The biggest motivator, cited by 40 percent, was a desire to work for themselves. An executive of the British Telecom unit that commissioned the poll said it showed "entrepreneurs seem to be snubbing the high risk 'get rich quick' career path in favor of a more realistic approach to running a business, designed to fit around their lifestyles and ages."[4]

I have conducted fairly in-depth interviews with hundreds, if not thousands, of small business owners. But for some reason, when the subject of independence comes up, I always recall a comment I overheard one day while I was in a plumbing supply house looking for a part to fix a leaky faucet. I was peering at the display of washer kits when a burly, mustachioed plumbing contractor answered a question from the cashier who was working the register.

"I work for m'self," he answered, in a strong voice that rang with pride, a fierce determination and a marked emphasis on the last syllable.

I had to turn around and look at him, because his simple answer to the question "Who do you work for?" made such a powerful personal statement about who he was, what he valued, and why he was in business. Did this guy have some horrible experience with an abusive boss that soured him forever on being an employee? Had his father or mother been an entrepreneur and ingrained in him from cradle days the importance of independence? I was not in journalist interview mode at the time and let him go without asking, so I'll never know. Maybe that's good because, stripped of detail, this one proudly autonomous individual has come to stand, to me, for all the entrepreneurs who are in business because they want to be their own bosses.

Personally, in conversation I tend to downplay the "I work for m'self" attitude. If somebody asks me who I work for, I am liable to admit to being unemployed, or semi-employed, before labeling myself as self-employed. But that's just my attempt at the social graces. The truth is, I am proud and grateful that I don't work for anybody. I chafe unbearably at supervision.

Working from Home

Not until 1992 did pollsters from the U.S. Census Bureau ask people it surveyed about their home-based businesses. Where have these head-counters been? Everybody knows that the chance to work from home is one of the prime seductions of self-employment. And since I started working full-time from home in 1987, home-based businesses have gone from odd to commonplace. Now, thanks to the bureau's survey, we have some authoritative numbers showing how important this lure is for entrepreneurs. What the 1992 Characteristics of Business Owners survey found was that almost half of the 17 million small businesses it identified were home-based.[5]

The Census Bureau didn't ask why these people worked from home. However, a number of other studies have shown several reasons why people want to labor in the same place they live. First on the list is the chance to care for young children. Moms whose lifestyle need is to stay home with their kids make up a large proportion of the lifestyle entrepreneurs out there. Of course, they're not all moms. Take Jon Sidoli.

Jon intended to get a job after selling his interest in the web consulting firm he cofounded. In the course of leading that business from zero to $600,000 a year in sales in only a year, he found that managing a fast-growing business was not his forte. He was actually looking forward to being an employee again. But after his wife took a job requiring a two-hour commute, he decided to come up with another new venture instead. This one would be home-based, specifically so he could be there to take care of the couple's elementary school–age daughter. "If I was working full-time, we'd have a day-care-and-dinner-at-eight-and-kiss-them-in-bed-when-they're-already-asleep situation," says the 50-year-old resident of Irvine, California. "I didn't think that was right."

Four years later, Jon's one-man enterprise advising school districts about the skills employers required of new workers brings in less than half the $125,000 income he was used to. He relies on his wife's earnings from her high-level job and, when he has to, dips into the six-figure sum banked from the sale of his former venture. But the lifestyle benefit has been more than enough to keep him from looking back with regret. "If you enjoy your family and being there for your daughter and you can make a few bucks," he says, "then you're fine."

Doing the Work You Love

Asked what makes a happy life, Sigmund Freud said, "To love and to work." How great could life be then, if you combined what you love with what you did for work? To be candid, it's also true that Freud warned against expecting too much of our happiness from one quarter. But that doesn't necessarily invalidate his love-and-work quote, nor does it mean that it's a bad idea to try to do work that makes you happy. And for lifestyle entrepreneurs, one of the big draws is the chance to start a business that can turn a hobby into a pastime, an avocation into a vocation.

Robin Knepp spent nine years in the Marine Corps, rising to the rank of captain as a logistics officer. "I did a lot of facilities management stuff, control of transportation assets, all the logistical functions to support the marines," Robin explains. "It's a very marketable skill." What lured Robin to leave the leathernecks wasn't a high-paying civilian job; instead, it was the opportunity to work full-time with dogs.

While still on active duty, Robin, a lifelong dog-lover, took a six-week canine training course and began training pets on the side. Business grew so much that when the inevitable transfer to a new Marine Corps post loomed, she opted to leave active duty and opened All About Dogs in Woodbridge, Virginia. Originally a home-based training service, she expanded it over eight years into a combination training and doggie day care facility with twelve employees.

Robin now gets to devote nearly full-time to her favorite activities: working with dogs and their owners, taking extended vacations with her own two dogs, and continuing to serve as a major in the Marine Corps Reserves. "That's a benefit too," she says of her lifestyle venture. "I can do some active duty without having to worry about leaving my job." Without lifestyle entrepreneurship, she'd likely still be a full-time marine, and she wouldn't be engaging in her other chosen pastimes nearly as much.

Places of the Heart

A lot of us have a place that is more special to us than any other. For me, it's probably New York City. I met my wife there, and our daughters were born there. It was also where I was first exposed to the workaday world of journalism during a summer spent in the Time-Life Building as a college intern in the fact-checking department of *People* magazine. For other people, that special place may be the beach, the mountains, a tropical isle, or a small town. Places of the heart are, naturally, as diverse as the longings of the people who love them. One thing many of these diverse places have in common is that, while they may be special to our hearts, they aren't kind to our wallets. Often, the problem is not that they are so expensive to live in, but that there is practically no way for us to get a job in them—or at least one that pays enough money to live on. For many people, the solution is to create a business that allows them to be where they want to be.

During my last semester of college, I applied for a job as a writer at *People*. Although I had never visited New York City or at that point considered it as a possible place to live, I had been taken in by the city's allure. As you might expect for a graduate of a big state school out West, I didn't get hired there. Instead, I did what a lot of cub reporters do: I went to work covering the police beat at a daily news-paper in a small city. I never forgot my desire to live in New York City, but the next few years of my career led me instead to Houston and then Dallas. New York, the media capital, seemed an inaccessible distance away from these comparative backwaters. Few journalists from Texas were able to make the leap to the big time, and I didn't think I had what it took to get hired by the *New York Times* or any other of the well-known media outlets there.

The key to New York City was my decision to become a lifestyle entrepreneur. As a self-employed journalist, I was free to live anywhere I wanted. The work is truly location-independent. Once you have clients, they don't care where you are. New York wasn't incompatible with freelance journalism—far from it. But the fact that I didn't need to get a new job to move to a new place meant I could indulge my preferences. And New York was my goal. Almost as soon as I started my lifestyle venture, I began plotting how to move. It took a while, because of some financial and personal entanglements that had to be dealt with. But three years after leaving my job, I left my home and family and friends behind and headed for Manhattan. I didn't know a soul, had no apartment to live in and no job, other than a small backlog of article assignments. I think it's safe to say that most of my friends and acquaintances in Texas considered my plan so clearly foolish that there was no need to even point out its folly. Yet it was probably the best move I've ever made in terms of lifestyle.

For months, I woke up every morning totally thrilled to be living in the city. Less than a year after moving there, I was shopping for a wedding ring. Three years later, I was witnessing the birth of my first daughter at Lenox Hill Hospital. Life-changing is too modest an adjective to describe the effects on my life of being able to live in that special place. And it was all due to my initiation of a lifestyle entrepreneur venture.

You can use a lifestyle venture as a lever to land you where you want to be even if you don't know exactly where that is or what you want to do when you get there. Thom Price had just graduated from college when he decided to try to get a fellowship for a year of independent study abroad. He didn't have any particular place or topic in mind until gondola-building occurred to him. "I knew I had it in the bag," Thom recalls. He also had a place—Venice, Italy—the one place in the world where the dying craft of building traditional handmade gondolas was still practiced. Thom funded his apprenticeship to an elderly master builder with the fellowship money, then started his own business in Venice. He spends 500 hours making each of his hand-built gondolas, then sells them, mostly to Americans, for $35,000 to $60,000 apiece. Thom not only makes a living and keeps a 900-year-old tradition alive, but he does it in one of the most beautiful tourist destinations in the world.[6]

A Workweek That Works

It's a truism that becoming an entrepreneur is synonymous with becoming a workaholic. "Be prepared to put in twelve-hour days to make it work," warns one popular entrepreneur's guide. That's pretty good advice, especially in the beginning. But it's not an inescapable fact that entrepreneurs work harder than everybody else. In fact, however, many lifestyle entrepreneurs work no harder than employees, and some work less.

One study by the National Federation of Independent Businesses (NFIB) of nearly 3,000 start-up entrepreneurs found that nearly one in four reported working fifty hours or less per week.[7] The average American worker puts in almost thirty-eight hours a week when averaged out over a year's time for vacation and other time off. The point is that entrepreneurs don't necessarily work that much harder than other workers. (They actually put in less time on the job than employees in Hong Kong, Singapore, and other East Asian countries put in, according to the International Labor Organization, which compiled the American employee workweek numbers as well.)

Keep in mind that these entrepreneurs get to have a lot of say in when and how they work. When you add vastly increased flexibility in choosing the time and type of work you do, it's no surprise that the opportunity to create a workweek that works is one of the basic appeals of the entrepreneurship lifestyle.

The NFIB study didn't ask whether any entrepreneurs worked fewer than forty hours or fewer than thirty hours. That first category includes me, because I typically labor thirty-five to forty hours a week. Another issue is whether lifestyle entrepreneurs are working more or less than they would in the type of jobs they might have if they were employed. In other words, it makes more sense to compare their current schedules to the way they worked as employees, rather than comparing them to the average employee. When I asked lifestyle entrepreneurs about their hours on the job, I found a significant number were putting in less time at work than when they were employees.

When Caryn Amherst was a corporate marketing director for a shopping mall operator, she routinely worked sixty to eighty hours a week. Nowadays, as president of Custom Marketing Associates of Elk Grove, Illinois, her home-based marketing consultancy, Caryn works a more reasonable schedule. More importantly, she controls how much and when she is on duty.

"Just because you are an entrepreneur does not mean that you can slack off or work less," she says. "But now I can choose the hours that I work." Sometimes she's still up at 3 A.M. working on a client project. But she also has time to attend events with her children and grandchildren. "I couldn't have done that before," she says.

Being able to choose how much and when to work is also important to Cheryl Leonhardt. She was a banker before she began a series of businesses revolving around the use of golf as a business tool. Now she consults with corporations, speaks, writes, and trains female executives in golfing for business. But only when she wants to. "I'm the best boss I ever had," says Cheryl. "If I want to quit at 2 o'clock and go to my golf club and practice at the range or play nine holes, that's fine."

Many lifestyle entrepreneurs hope to do something that few employees can dream of: eventually reducing their workweeks to part-time levels. Anne Warfield, who runs a home-based Minneapolis training and public speaking company with her husband, Paul Cummings, says her husband used to come home from his job at 6:30 P.M. every workday. "We now go into work at 8:30 and leave by 4:30 and have dinner with the kids," she says. "We're at all their major events. My husband has had flexible time to be home with the kids during my pregnancies. We can take time off. And our ultimate goal is to work thirty hours a week."

Some lifestyle entrepreneurs have already reached that goal, and beyond. After her daughter was born, Elise Goldstein left her full-time job at a public relations firm to set up a freelance media relations business out of her Louisville home. "I make about half as much, but instead of working an eight-hour day, I work about two hours while my daughter sleeps," Elise says. Note that she's working a quarter as much, but earning half as much. That's because she charges more as an independent than her employer paid her. Additional work is available at those rates should she choose to take it on. "If I wanted to," Elise says, "I could work more hours after she went to bed and then make as much as I was before."

Burying the Road Warrior Hatchet

Dave Jacobs knew he was in trouble when, he says, "The Hertz guy in Atlanta was my best friend." That might have been fine, except Dave was living in Houston at the time. Working as a consultant for a large technology consulting company often meant he was in an airplane five nights a week, away from family, away from his home, and away from his life. "There was something badly wrong. I wanted out," Dave recalls.

He left the company in 1996, along with a like-minded colleague, and formed his own firm, TechKnowledge Consulting Corporation. The idea was to do the same work, with one major difference: The Houston-based company would take no clients located outside of Texas. Given the concentration of technology consulting prospects in the state's major cities—none more than an hour away from Houston by air and all well-served by frequent, sometimes hourly flights—this business model meant Dave would never have to spend another night away from home.

Whether it would provide him with enough clients to make a go of it was another thing. As it turned out, Dave had enough in-state business—and then some—to keep him and his partner busy. TechKnowl-edge now has offices in Houston, Dallas, Fort Worth, and Austin, and Dave finds himself presiding over a multimillion-dollar business. Through it all, he has kept the in-state criterion for all clients and stayed focused on the reasons he started the company in the first place. One of the keys that has helped him grow the company has been the availability—indeed, the eagerness—of additional seasoned technology consultants to join him.

"I didn't particularly care if this was financially successful," he says. "But it turns out that there are a whole lot of people in the tech business who enjoy doing what we do, but they don't want to live their lives out of a suitcase." Amen to that.

Taming the Tech Beast

In one of my first jobs as a reporter, we wrote our stories on flimsy buff-colored copy paper fed through the platens of electric typewriters and delivered them—suitably speckled with pencil scratchings, taped-on insertions, and daubed correction fluid—to a typesetter who keyed the words into a machine that transformed them into lead type, which was used to print the paper. They don't do it that way anymore. Even before I got out of college, the use of electronic terminals connected to computerized phototypesetters was standard.

(Although, a few conservative outfits clung to their typewriters. At my very first paid journalism gig as a *People* intern, only the lowly typing pool used word processors. We in the research department had up-to-date electric typewriters; the more senior writers used progressively less modern equipment, until you got to the managing editor, who banged out copy on an antique manual Underwood with a wooden space bar.)

Nowadays, I'm sure you'd be hard-pressed to find any publication whose employees used typewriters for much more than addressing express package labels. Personally, I think that's an improvement. I like computers, and I like writing on computers, doing research on them, and just generally playing around with them. Not everybody feels that way. Some people just don't like that level of technology. When you add cell phones, pagers, wireless handheld e-mail terminals, laptop PCs, personal digital assistants, and the other technological paraphernalia of modern working life, the number of people who are at least moderately interested in getting away from all these gadgets grows significantly.

Good luck if you want to tame the tech beast while working for a company. Modern offices are so full of information technology that the industry has hit a sales slump because virtually every conceivable info-need is already being met by installed hardware. It's no better if you work out of the office or travel a lot. Being chained to a pager, clipped to a cell phone, and shackled to a laptop is pretty much the universal experience for mobile workers these days.

That's why you have to like Kirkpatrick Sale. He is a freelance writer and contributing editor at *The Nation* as well as author of a number of books, including *Rebels Against the Future: The Luddites and Their War on the Industrial Revolution: Lessons for the Computer Age* (Perseus Publishing, 1996). While his writing covers many topics, a recurring theme is a reluctance to embrace technology as fully as the rest of modern society seems to have done. While he's not as radical as the loom-smashing Luddites, he does call out for intellectual revolt against what he sees as the tyranny of technology. That's gotten him lambasted in *Wired* magazine and critically examined in the *New York Times,* the *New Yorker,* and other publications. But it hasn't swayed Kirkpatrick.

"I use a typewriter," he says, "and I write a lot on top of the page as it's going through the machine, doing my editing with pen or pencil." Kirkpatrick says the choice of the tools he uses in his self-employment lifestyle reflects "an entirely personal response to the tools of your life. There are lots of people who like the feel of pencils, in particular. They like to see the strokes of writing and feel the paper under their hand."[8]

The desire to escape their electronic leashes led some lifestyle entrepreneurs to pursue their ventures. "I always had a beeper and was always on call," Caryn Amherst says of her life as a corporate employee before setting up her own marketing company. Beeper backlash is a perfectly good reason to set up a lifestyle business. When you're the boss, you don't have to worry about whether being available twenty-four hours a day is a job requirement or merely something that looks good. You can do it or not, according to the real needs of the enterprise.

Working with People You Like

Book publicity agency owner Lynn Goldberg, who retains my wife, Barbara Cave Henricks, as vice president and director of the company's business division, has a track record of hiring straight-A graduates of Ivy League schools to fill entry level positions at her small New York City firm. She also has a reputation of offering a wonderful place to work, and the young publicists who come to work for her frequently move on after a few years to top publicity and marketing jobs at leading New York publishing houses.

I don't know Lynn all that well, which may be why I was surprised to hear that her basic rule about hiring people is to only take on people she would like to have dinner with. How can this apparent penchant for hard-driving high performance and for people who can stand the pace be reconciled with a criterion such as "only people you'd have dinner with"? If you met many of the ten or so employees of Goldberg McDuffie Communications, you would be struck by how friendly, considerate, and downright charming they all are. Although very smart and productive to a person, they are precisely the sort who make excellent company.

In that, they are quite different from the run of employees of most large corporations, especially those in deadline-driven, results-oriented fields such as book publicity. Lynn's insistence on working only with people she would like to work with makes her an example of a special kind of lifestyle entrepreneur, the kind who goes into business so he or she can exercise greater control over the human environment at work. Some lifestyle entrepreneurs prefer their own company, so they design ventures that place them alone during much, if not all, of the workday. Others accomplish the difficult but rewarding challenge of mingling marriage with career, crafting enterprises in which they can partner with a spouse.

Lifestyle entrepreneurs are also motivated by the desire to work with customers and suppliers they like. Maryalice Hurst gave up a high-profile advertising career after surviving cancer treatment that included a bone marrow transplant. "Having been that sick and seeing so many people die, I really didn't want to sell soap for the rest of my life," Maryalice says. "Also in the early 1980s, I became aware of the abuse of consumer data by large insurance companies, banks, you name it. People taking data that had been offered for one purpose and applying it for another." After trying out several alternatives to continuing to play the same game with people whose motives she had come to disrespect, she wound up moving from a Connecticut suburb of New York City to Conway, Arkansas, and opening a bookstore.

Doing Work That Matters

What kind of work matters? That's a difficult question for anybody to answer. For Michelle Paster, it was helping special children learn. That was the kind of work she found meaningful in her former job as a Boston-area public school teacher. "It is very rewarding," Michelle says. "And when you're successful with a kid, it's a great feeling." Dealing with the bureaucracy of a public school system took her away from that, and that's why in 1999 she quit the school system to start LearningWorks Inc., a one-person enterprise that teaches children to deal with their learning disabilities, trains teachers, and consults with school districts. Working on her own allows her to focus on teaching kids rather than shuttling them from grade to grade, Michelle explains. "The nice thing is, now I stay with kids for extended periods of time," she says. "I'll stay with kids for years."

You don't have to be a teacher to find work that matters. Lifestyle entrepreneurs find meaning designing web pages, raising money for charities, and many other activities. Some of them are able to inject special meaning into what may seem like mundane businesses by performing pro bono work for causes they have selected.

If you talk to enough lifestyle business owners about why they do what they do, you'll begin to get the feeling that there are as many reasons as there are entrepreneurs. That is probably not far from the truth. Kristin Rhyne is one example. She is a former investment banker who started her venture, an airport beauty spa concept called Polished Inc., while she was attending Harvard Business School. Although during its three years Polished has grown to employ fifteen people, Kristin says that there is no comparison to her pre-entrepreneur income. "I went from making a nice banking paycheck to making no paycheck for about a year and a half," she says. "And it's still substantially reduced."

Kristin takes compensatory pleasure in the equity she is building in a venture she conceived and runs hands-on. But the real reason she does it, she says, is for the challenge. "For me, starting this company was not a career move," says Kristin. "I don't make career moves. I go after challenges. And this happened to be the next challenge in my life."

Imagining the Ideal Life

The next challenge in your own odyssey to become a lifestyle entrepreneur is to imagine the ideal life. Start by asking yourself, "What do I do for fun?" Fun activities may seem unlikely sources for potential business ideas. However, people have found ways to create businesses out of the wackiest pastimes and hobbies, even those with seemingly no potential for commercialization. Jeremy, my niece's boyfriend, enjoyed a role-playing fantasy card game called Magic: The Gathering. He was good at it, too—enough that his team took second place in an international Magic: The Gathering tournament and wound up on the cover of a hobbyist magazine devoted to the game. But what was really interesting about Jeremy was the way he was able to turn his hobby into a part-time business.

One key to playing the game is collecting various cards that represent powerful weapons, protective armor, useful tools, and the like. These help the characters navigate the many dangers in the game. Because of his skill, Jeremy was able to gather many hard-to-get and potent cards. He found that other players were willing to pay cash for some of them, and he was a willing seller. Eventually, by trading and selling sought-after cards, he generated income adequate to provide significant financial assistance to a college student, which he was at the time.

If Jeremy can make a business from a fantasy role-playing card game, it's hard to say what might not make a viable business. Indeed, I have heard of people who created lifestyle businesses from alpaca farming, trading obsolete eight-track tape players and cartridges, and even making buggy whips. One of the most far-fetched business ideas I ever ran across was a Sonoma, California, management consulting firm run by a designer and woodworker who taught entrepreneurs to understand their companies by modeling their business plans in clay. As in sculpting clay. No spreadsheets, no mission statements, and no kidding. Some of his students swore by it. So whatever it is that you do for fun, take a look at turning it into a business. It's hard to rule anything out.

Starting with Anything Is Possible

When you begin contemplating a major change such as starting a business, the initial thrill of excitement is often followed by the chill of confusion, negativism, or downright depression. That can happen when you naturally—but prematurely—begin critiquing your ideas, subjecting them to your internal devil's advocate and, in essence, shooting them down before they ever get a chance to become airborne.

While it's important that your thinking about lifestyle entrepreneurship ultimately be grounded in reality, it's probably a mistake to be too hard on your dreams at this point. In fact, it's a good idea to start by assuming anything is possible. I haven't met any lifestyle entrepreneurs who started researching their successful ventures with a long list of can'ts. It may be true that you can't do a lot of stuff, but now is not the time to focus on that.

Start your search for a lifestyle venture by removing all boundaries to your imagination. Do not say, for instance, "I'm not very good at X" or "I don't have any connections to Y" or "I'm flat out of money and I have zero experience at Z so I can't even think about doing what I want." That's not the way to go about it. Instead, decide what you want in an open, anything-is-possible manner. Then think about finding a way to do what you want.

Maybe you think this is a foolish, Pollyanna attitude. It's not. For example, what would you say to someone who wanted to become a book publisher when he didn't enjoy reading, rarely read more than a couple of paragraphs at a time and, in fact, had never read the first book he published? Would you say he's crazy?

If you told Tim McCormick that prior to his founding of Greentree Publishing of Tempe, Arizona, he would probably have ignored you. And he would have been right to do so. Tim started his lifestyle venture in 1998 specifically because he wanted to publish a book by a certain speaker he'd heard at a parenting seminar. "I didn't even read his book until a year and a half after I published it," Tim admits. "I'm just not much of a reader. One or two paragraphs is enough for me." However, things worked out. *How to Behave So Your Kids Will Too*, by Sal Severe, was a major success, selling several hundred thousand copies. If a reluctant reader like Tim can publish a best-seller on his first try, you can succeed in spite of your limitations as well.

By encouraging lifestyle entrepreneurship, I'm not advocating tossing caution to the wind, quitting your job, and taking out a second mortgage to pursue the first appealing business idea that pops into your head. Later we'll discuss precisely what the chances are that your venture will not succeed. You'll probably find that starting a small business is not as risky as you thought. Still, due diligence must be exercised. There is a lot at stake here. If you torch your career and drain your retirement accounts in a vain effort to create a business that you could have known in advance was unlikely to succeed, it is not going to do anything for your lifestyle. You can learn a lot from mistakes, to be sure. But that is no reason to increase the likelihood of making mistakes by acting precipitously.

Before you commit your career, your finances, and your life to a lifestyle venture, you have to have some degree of reality-based confidence that it will succeed. There's no such thing as a sure thing in business, of course. Even the most well-financed, carefully researched, and exhaustively planned ventures can and do sometimes fail to make it far out of the starting blocks. Your lifestyle venture will inevitably involve a leap of faith of some distance. Just make sure that you have a reasonable chance of clearing the gap.

Maintaining a Lifestyle Focus

Once you get into the world of business, it can be seductive. Although you may have started your study of lifestyle entrepreneurship with the goal of living in the mountains or spending more time with your children, before long you may find yourself addled by all the talk of price points and marketing plans, shareholder's equity and loan covenants. You may start buying into the idea that bigger is better, busier is happier, and that no sacrifice of lifestyle is too great to grow faster and increase margins. You may, in short, become a stereotypical entrepreneur—an animal we have already seen is not the typical entrepreneur.

It's certainly possible to have a successful business without sacrificing lifestyle considerations. Jane Pollak has been in business as an egg decorator for thirty years, but still isn't sure exactly how she became an entrepreneur. "It was part of who I was," says Jane. "I didn't say, 'I'm in business. This is what I do, here's my card.' I started doing something I love and found I could make money at it."

Because the issues with lifestyle entrepreneurship are so different from strictly commercial ventures, this book doesn't deal with all the regular start-a-business issues. If you want to learn more about growth, financing, marketing, and other entrepreneurial matters, I've included a list of recommended books, web sites, periodicals, and other resources in the Appendix. While few deal specifically with lifestyle needs, all are good sources of general business know-how that will do a lot to help you see that the bottom-line performance of your company is adequate to support your lifestyle requirements.

While you're looking through some of those more traditional entrepreneurship manuals, don't neglect the essential component of imagination when it comes to creating your lifestyle business. For someone brought up in a conventional existence, it takes a prodigious ability to imagine the ideal life—to see the possibilities in Maryalice Hurst's trade of Madison Avenue for Main Street or in any of the other courageous and slightly crazy plunges taken by lifestyle entrepreneurs. If you're going to follow Ron Kipp's giant stride into madness, make sure you take your imagination with you when you step off the edge.

TWO

Looking in the Mirror

D o you have what it takes to be a lifestyle entrepreneur? The only
good answer to this question is the one that will occur to you
many years from now as you look back on a long career as a successful lifestyle business owner. At that point, you can say, "Yes, based on
the fact that I ran this operation for twenty years and made a living
and had a fine time doing it, it appears that I did have what it takes to
be a lifestyle entrepreneur." From our current perspective, it's not so
straightforward. There is no checklist of characteristics that you can
go through—placing a number from one to five (depending on how
strongly you feel you match the given trait), adding them together at
the end and, if your score is over thirty, knowing for sure you are a
born lifestyle entrepreneur.

Checklists and score sheets are not useless. However, they are not
definitive determinants of what it takes to be an entrepreneur, and
they shouldn't be treated that way. Decisiveness is a common component of these traits-of-an-entrepreneur lists. It's said that you must be
able to swiftly and surely make decisions if you are to make it as an
entrepreneur. But what about the many lifestyle entrepreneurs who
waffle for years over whether or not to take the plunge into lifestyle
business ownership? That group includes me. I consider myself a successful lifestyle entrepreneur, and yet I was unable to make the most
important decision of all over a long period of time.

Jim and Tatia Rauch had a similar experience. "For years we had dreamed about moving to Sedona, Arizona," Jim says. "We had vacationed there many, many times in the seven years we have known each other. We got engaged there. We got married there. Our hearts—and our hiking boots—were rooted there. But how to make a living there—that was the big question." Lack of an answer blocked the Rauches for years and kept them from deciding to cut the ties that bound them to their corporate existences in Southern California. Yet, despite this lack of entrepreneurial decisiveness, they eventually did move to Sedona, opened the Adobe Hacienda bed-and-breakfast, and settled into the dream that—maybe because it took so long to bring to reality—turned out to be even sweeter than they had imagined.

"Though it has been a lot of work and it is a seven-day-a-week job, we've never regretted the decision," says Jim. "We love where we are, what we do, and our resort lifestyle. We like to say it seems like every day is Sunday. Other people say we had real courage to take the chance and make such a radical lifestyle change. But, for us, it's exciting. It's fun. It's exactly what we wanted to do with our lives. People ask if there's anything we miss about our old lives, about California. We just smile and say, 'No!'"

The many successful stories of lifestyle entrepreneurship told by people like the Rauches make it tough to say that you have to be decisive or brilliant or take-charge or even determined. Jane Pollak says she just fell into her business while doing what she enjoyed as a hobby. Rather than trying to force lifestyle entrepreneurs to conform to a preconceived set of personality traits, I prefer to take an open-minded look at the topic and see how many different personality types can turn into successful lifestyle entrepreneurs. It's a big group that covers a broad spectrum.

The Role of Role Models

Lifestyle entrepreneurship hasn't been a popular subject of scientific study to date, so there are few hard numbers to go on when you're trying to track the trend and identify popular motivations and successful tactics. What we do have are a lot of people. Lifestyle entrepreneurs themselves, telling their stories and relating their tips and tricks, are the best available exemplars and instructors we have. Fortunately, actual examples have a powerful capacity for teaching and inspiring lifestyle business owners.

Knowing about a successful entrepreneur makes it more likely that you'll not only try but succeed in a similar endeavor yourself, according to William D. Bygrave, head of the well-regarded entrepreneurship center at Babson College. Writing in *The Portable MBA in Entrepreneurship* (Wiley, 1994), Professor Bygrave says such environmental factors that exist in the outside world may be as important to entrepreneurs as the so-called entrepreneurial traits that they carry within. The significance of environmental factors is shown by the clumping of start-up businesses in such places as Silicon Valley and Boston's Route 128 high-tech community, he says.

Many people have never encountered the idea of creating a business that addresses lifestyle needs before financial ones. For them, learning of the possibility of lifestyle entrepreneurship is a necessary first step to deciding whether or not it is for them. If they don't even know it's an option, how can they choose it? For other people, including those who already regard starting a business as central to their lifestyle solution, learning about thriving lifestyle ventures reinforces their sense of the viability of the entrepreneur lifestyle, as well as providing anecdotal evidence of the validity of different ways to go about it.

So when you read about lifestyle entrepreneurs and feel a thrill of identification and an urge to emulate their behavior, don't be too skeptical about the worth of your sensations. This is no mere voyeurism. You may be learning exactly what you need from these stories of entrepreneurs who created new and more appealing lives along with their new enterprises.

So, who, generally, are lifestyle entrepreneurs? The easy answer is that they come in countless varieties. It's a little harder, but much more useful, to try to separate them into different categories such as midcareer burnouts, parents of young children, recently laid-off or downsized workers, or those facing some kind of unacceptable workplace condition, such as a transfer to an undesirable locale. You may see yourself as a member of one of these groups. If not, don't despair. There are more kinds of lifestyle entrepreneurs than have been cataloged to date, certainly, and more are being born all the time.

Burned-Out Mid-Careerist

There's not much doubt that among the most likely candidates for lifestyle entrepreneurship are people who have worked for several years as corporate employees, put aside a certain amount of savings or other assets, and, in the process, got thoroughly sick of the whole scene. These burned-out mid-careerists have usually been moderately successful in their line of work, and sometimes extraordinarily so. Yet there is something about what they do that has come to chafe at them. It may be office politics, corporate bureaucracy, or nothing specific. What is important is that after what may be ten, twenty, or more years of doing very much the same kind of work, they feel the time has come for a change.

Bill Baker is a typical example. In 1998, he was a top account executive for a public relations agency, with IBM Corp. as his main client. The job involved a lot of travel and evenings spent recuperating in hotels after ten- and eleven-hour workdays. "The money was good," Bill recalls. "The lifestyle was not." He also disliked the endless meetings, memos, planning sessions, and e-mails covering memos about planning session meetings. "I felt I was spending more time talking about the job as opposed to doing the job," he says. "I'm not big on that. I'm big on sitting down, deciding what needs to be done, and doing it."

So Bill left the agency in May of that year, despite a fat salary increase dangled by the owner, and opened his own communications agency in New Milford, Connecticut. "I had no clients and, basically, nothing," Bill says. "It was totally a lifestyle decision. Happily, it turned out great and I'm making a nice living."

These mid-career burnouts tend to have a few more things in common. Often they have amassed fairly comfortable piles of savings, enough to help them get their lifestyle venture off the ground, if not enough to make them financially independent. Frequently they work in fields where start-up costs are relatively low, such as consulting and professional services. Always, they have the willingness to embrace business ownership as a way out of the blind alley they have worked their way into.

"I did it because I wanted to do something different, says Patricia Joyce, who was a California banking executive before she became owner of The Duke of Windsor Inn in Cape May, New Jersey. "I was very good at what I did," Patricia says, "but I felt like I wanted to try something different. I wanted to develop other skills, and I wanted to do something entrepreneurial. I also wanted to live by the beach. So, here I am."

Special Lifestyle Needs

A second big group of lifestyle entrepreneurs are those I broadly lump together as having special lifestyle needs. They include parents of young children, grown children of elderly parents, people who have health problems, and those who have an ailing or disabled family member. They also include those who want to work alongside a spouse or other family member instead of joining the general workforce. For these people, entrepreneurship is often the only conceivable way they could meet their needs for flexible schedules, special locations, and the right to choose who they work with.

A measure of controversy surrounds the concept of women starting businesses so they can work from home and care for their young children. For instance, when the Center for Women's Business Research presented a 1995 study showing that women owners of home-based businesses were no more likely to have children at home than non-home-based women business owners, the Washington, D.C.-based organization said the finding "contradicts the supposition that women base careers from home to balance the needs of work and a young family."[1] With all due respect, I don't see the contradiction. Going further, I can state as a fact that many women (and men and couples too) do specifically start home-based businesses so they can spend more time with their kids. The good news is, it works.

Patti Glick worked as a nurse at a podiatric practice and enjoyed the work. But when her twins were about to start school, a change was in order. "I decided that I wanted to be home to help them with their homework," she says. "I didn't want to send them to day care, not when it came to homework habits. So I decided to be a stay-at-home mom."

Soon after quitting her job, Patti realized that there was an opportunity to start a part-time business giving educational seminars about foot health to local companies. "I could go and teach people during the lunch hour and still be at home when my kids get home," she figured. So she started a one-person home-based business called The Foot Nurse. That was in 1996; five years later, she was earning up to $600 a day giving a brown-bag seminar followed by a foot-measurement clinic. She works a few more hours than she used to, but she makes a good living and she's still able to spend more time with the twins than she could have as a full-time nurse. "It's been a very nice blend," she says.

I could not make a convincing argument that women are less business-minded than men, even if I believed it. I've been exposed to far too many thoroughly worldly and sophisticated female entrepreneurs. However, taken as a group and without comparing them to men, it does seem that women entrepreneurs are likely to have lifestyle goals in mind. Here's what one Australian study of women-owned small businesses found: "The results revealed that women tend to pursue small business as a lifestyle choice. Although different women seek different lifestyles, ultimately the question of growth of the business is pinned to lifestyle issues such as balance and flexibility."[2]

Men and couples can and do also start businesses to make it easier to care for their children. Canadians Cathy-Ann Glockner and Kelly Toole started a business making and selling an all-natural body cleanser called Cathy-Ann's Kootenay Coconut Soap in their Nelson, British Columbia, home so they could both stay home with the couple's two young children. The two are committed to a natural, low-impact alternative lifestyle in addition to being committed to raising their kids. Their lifestyle enterprise allows them to do both. "We're trying to live what we preach, and if anyone else is inspired by what we do, then that's great too," says Cathy-Ann. "I'm thrilled we can make a living from soap. But I'm even more glad that we can raise our kids together. They're going to remember that when they were growing up, mom and dad were at home."[3]

The flip side of lifestyle entrepreneurship is that it can allow you to spend more time with mom and dad. Ann Dennis and her husband grew up in Richardson, Texas, a Dallas suburb, before moving to the Pacific Northwest to embark on successful careers as high-tech executives. When their parents, who all still lived in the Dallas area, began to get on in years, they both felt they wanted to be closer so they could spend time with them. "That was a major driving force to move back," says Ann. "If we wait, then what? What have you lost?"

After their son graduated from high school and began spending a lot of time in Texas, they decided there were no more reasons to stay in Oregon. They both quit their jobs, returned to Dallas, and eventually purchased a combination bed-and-breakfast and engraving business in Denison, just four miles from Lake Texoma, a giant man-made body of water straddling the Oklahoma border.

It wasn't a moment too soon. The Dennises moved from Oregon to Texas in January 1998, and that October her 94-year-old father passed away. "He took a really sudden turn for the worse, and I would never have been able to make it back in time," Ann recalls. "As it was, I saw him the first day he was admitted to the hospital, and I spent day and night there. I would never have been able to do that if we hadn't moved. For us, we definitely made the right decision."

Lifestyle entrepreneurship is also seen as a solution by people troubled with their own infirmities. "I don't know if you've ever met anybody who's had a bone marrow transplant," Maryalice Hurst says, "but afterward I just didn't have the drive to run a major subsidiary of something like Young & Rubicam."

During her lengthy recovery, Maryalice had been in virtual isolation, wearing a mask to shield her suppressed immune system and seeing almost no one but her husband and her doctors. "You come out of that environment onto the streets in New York and it's putrefying," she says. "Odors you never noticed before are very pungent. I found that unnerving. The noise of the horns blowing all the time drove me nuts. I'd lived in that environment for twenty years, was taken away from it, and when I was put back, I knew that was an environment I didn't want to live in anymore."

Pam Lontos is another lifestyle entrepreneur whose health problems were all she needed to convince her to investigate business ownership. Following a career with the Disney Corporation that saw her rise to the position of vice president of sales for the broadcasting unit, Pam hit the road as a hard-traveling sales and motivation speaker. Five years into her career, she fell and injured her back. But she continued to work.

"For the next thirteen years, the constant travel made it impossible for my injury to really heal," she says. "I got so burned-out on traveling that I decided that I had to make a change in order to improve my life." She and her husband started an Orlando, Florida, public relations firm for professional speakers. "Now I don't have to travel except for a few conferences, my back is vastly improved, and my life is mine again," she says. "I'm only sorry I took so long to make the change."

Laid Off, Downsized, or Fired

You're going to read a lot in this book about the wisdom of planning and patience when it comes to starting a lifestyle entrepreneur venture. But sometimes events overtake us and before we are ready or have even contemplated change, it is upon us. People who have been laid off or otherwise terminated, who expect to be let go soon, or who face unacceptable conditions of employment such as a cut in pay often see lifestyle entrepreneurship as a solution to their quandary. If you're one of these people, you already have one of the primary requirements of a potential lifestyle business owner—namely, a willingness to consider radical change because you're already going through a change, like it or not.

For Jim and Tatia Rauch, who had dreamed for years of moving from Southern California to Sedona, Arizona, the tipping point occurred when Jim lost his job. Tatia had always wanted to emulate her grandmother, who ran a country inn in Indiana. Jim liked that idea too, though he wasn't planning to do it anytime soon. "We always thought of it as a retirement scenario," he said. "But when I was suddenly laid off of my job, the time had come to decide what to do next with our lives.

"It was almost a natural choice for us consider purchasing and operating a bed and breakfast in Sedona," Jim says. "All the pieces fit. I could work at home doing what I love—taking care of and improving our home—as well as continue doing marketing—only now for myself—while Tatia could finally have the bed-and-breakfast to run that she'd always dreamed of." Before becoming a full-time parent, Tatia had worked in the tour industry and for several large hotels, so she had the background to make a go of it. "We both could be home twenty-four hours a day with our now three-year-old to enjoy family time seven days a week. And we could go hiking in the beautiful red rocks every single day!" Jim says.

Another common qualification for lifestyle entrepreneurship is that you and your current employer no longer see eye to eye. You may be facing a threat of being laid off, unacceptable employment conditions, a change in duties, or a cut in pay. Excessive travel in a corporate job is a common motivation for lifestyle entrepreneurs. Sometimes it's not so much the travel as the fact that you're going to have to transfer to an unacceptable location.

Marine Captain Robin Knepp, who was discussed in the previous chapter, was spurred to leave active duty by a looming assignment to a new post. While she loved the Corps, Robin didn't want leave behind the part-time dog training business she had started on the side. "It got to the point where I was going to get orders and have to move," she says. "So I decided to go into the reserves. And the only reason I got out was because of my business."

If your employer is engaging in some behavior that you don't care for, it can be important motivation for exploring lifestyle entrepreneurship. Maybe I'm not up on the moral state of employers today, but I have been surprised by the number of lifestyle business owners who told me they became entrepreneurs because of what they viewed as unethical practices or treacherous behavior by their former employers. Recall Maryalice Hurst, whose discomfort with the way her employers were handling sensitive customer data led her to leave the industry where she had built a stellar career.

Another example is Greentree Publishing founder and CEO Tim McCormick. Tim made good money in his old job, where he was a top sales rep in a company that had 700 of them. But the big payoff he was working toward was a chance to score in an Initial Public Offering of stock. "The whole pitch was, they'd build the company up and go public and everybody would do really well," Tim recalls. "But the owner turned on everybody and sold the company to another company for $380 million." Tim's frustration and disappointment spurred him to explore business ownership as a way to enforce his own standards on the way he did business.

Sometimes you may see a lifestyle entrepreneur in the mirror if the face looking back at you is about to retire. Dr. Charles Thomas spent thirty-two years as an Indiana obstetrician/gynecologist before retiring in 1994 to devote himself full-time to the small winery he had started as a part-time, two-person operation in an Indianapolis office-warehouse complex ten years earlier. Dr. Thomas is a classic lifestyle entrepreneur because he had not one, but several impulses pushing him toward owning a small business for lifestyle reasons.

To begin with, he loved wine. After getting started making wine at home in 1970 using a kit purchased at a local wine store, he progressed steadily in passion, skill, and ambition. Several years into it, he found himself flying to California each fall and bringing back as much grape juice as he could carry onto an airliner. Then he started working with a commercial source to get frozen pressed grapes and juice, and he began turning out fifty-gallon batches of cabernet, merlot, and other wines. He loved hanging out with wine makers and wine lovers, and enjoyed honing his skill.

An increasing dislike of changes in the medical field was another force, pushing him from behind. "It was getting more and more difficult to practice medicine with the HMOs paying you thirty-five cents on the dollar and telling you you can't do something for your patients that you know you should do," he said. "I decided I didn't need this, so I retired from medicine and came to the winery full-time."

Dr. Thomas is a man of firm opinions who doesn't flinch from controversy and, in fact, seems to relish a challenge. Inevitably, he felt convinced he could make better wines than those being created by established Indiana vintners. "You get to the point where your ego says you can make better wine than so-and-so down the road who has a commercial winery," he says. "So I decided to start a commercial winery."

Chateau Thomas Winery allowed him to express his personality through wine making. He didn't care for wines made with the American varieties of grapes; he preferred the fruit of French-style vinifera vines that were unable to withstand the harsh Indiana winters. So he invariably imported grapes and juice from California and other sources. The practice irritated other Indiana vintners who used local produce, but to Dr. Thomas it proved a point, in addition to producing consistently prize-winning wines.

Making wine also appealed because it was so different from the practice of medicine. "I liked wine making because it was something that would wait for you," he says. "It isn't something you have to do today." Once a year, in the fall when the grapes come in, he's very busy pressing, fermenting, and barreling the vintages. "But then for some wines, it's three years in the barrel," he says, "You come in and taste them and make sure everything's okay, but it's not full-time."

Dr. Thomas's single biggest qualification for entrepreneurship was the irresistible appeal that his chosen business had from a lifestyle standpoint. "I like good food, and I like good wines. And I like the lifestyle that you get at a winery. I like the people that you meet. At this point in time, I have achieved enough notoriety in Indianapolis and central Indiana that a lot of people know who I am and what I do. When I see people that recognize me, we talk about wine. And I like that. It's nice for people to recognize what your passion is and to talk to you about your passion."

THREE

Recognizing the Limits

People told me not to write this chapter. "You're just undermining your message," they said, looking at me pityingly as if I just didn't get it. I get it all right, but I disagree that pointing out the risks, limitations, and costs of something is the same as undermining it. To me, being open and honest builds credibility. Perhaps it is my journalistic background, but my approach to studying and reporting on a topic is to walk all the way around it, seeing it from all sides and passing on my candid observations.

I'm not inflexible in this regard. When writing the freelance article proposals known as query letters, I refrain from mentioning anything that might cause the editor I am pitching to regard the article as anything other than scintillating and me as less than the perfect writer to handle the job. In the writing workshops I conduct, I repeat this admonition probably to the point of being boring, or even beyond. Query letters, however, are one thing. Honesty is not. Proposals are sales tools. This book is not. It's an attempt to report, analyze, and make recommendations on a fascinating life option that, in my opinion, too few people consider.

Lifestyle entrepreneurship does indeed have risks, limits, and costs. It would be unrealistic and misleading to present it otherwise. If you're going to make a good decision as to whether owning a lifestyle business is a good move for you, you need accurate information about the downside as well as the upside. So, here's the downside.

The Costs of Cutting Loose

The price of freedom may or may not include eternal vigilance when it comes to lifestyle entrepreneurship. But there's no doubt that the independence of business ownership does come at a price. Actually, there are several prices. You are likely to experience a cut in pay, at least initially. You will have to pay more taxes, generally—although in the United States at least you'll also often get additional deductions that may more than balance the ledger. And there are many other costs, ranging from the burden of being personally responsible for everything to the loss of the employer-provided extras such as health insurance and paid vacations that many people have come to expect as fringe benefits of working for a living.

Understanding the costs is an essential part of figuring out whether or not it will be worth it for you to consider lifestyle entrepreneurship. I don't know about you, but when I go into a restaurant and receive a menu without prices on it, I become wary. Likewise, the display case of a jeweler who carefully tucks the price tags behind the rings and bracelets is likely to receive no more than a cursory look from me. The old saying to the contrary, until you know what things cost, it's hard to figure out their value.

Most of the lifestyle entrepreneurs I've spoken to report bringing home smaller paychecks as early-stage entrepreneurs than they did as employees. That in itself isn't surprising. After all, these people by definition aren't in it for the money. On the other hand, this book is not intended for the financially independent. I'm assuming readers need income from their lifestyle businesses in order to survive. So it's entirely appropriate to ask: How much less can I expect to make?

Rather than spend paragraphs hemming and hawing about how it all depends, I will say that a 30 percent pay cut the first year is typical of what I hear. Some people experience bigger cuts, some smaller, some none, and some make more as lifestyle entrepreneurs than they did as employees.

Personally, it wasn't bad for me. In 1986 my job as an assistant newspaper editor paid $26,390. In 1987, the year I became a lifestyle entrepreneur, I grossed $25,539, a difference of less than 4 percent. The reason I didn't feel the same impact was that I'd spent five years working at writing part-time while getting ready financially, professionally, and emotionally to make the change. By the end of the first full year of lifestyle entrepreneurship, I was making more than I had in my old job. Today I earn more than I ever expected to as a journalist and writer. And, according to the salary surveys I have seen, that is significantly more than I could have hoped to earn if I'd kept on the career track.

I'm not the only one who has been pleasantly surprised by lifestyle entrepreneurship's financial rewards. Erin Allen bailed out of an eighteen-year career as a court reporter to open the Mango Inn, a bed-and-breakfast in Lake Worth, Florida. "Our inn is doing incredibly well," she reports. "It has surpassed my expectations as far as financial security."

There's another way things can play out. Listen to Wendy White, who quit practicing law in 1995 to open an outdoor adventure guide company and rustic lodge with her husband:

> The first year was fun and exciting, although we drained down all our financial resources and went into incredible debt because the business just didn't get off the ground as fast as we planned. The second year was still fun, but the anxiety of having no income and having to sell our last piece of income property to pay our overhead was overwhelming. The third year we began to wonder if we made the right choice as credit cards became our primary method of financing the monthly cash flow problems. The fourth year we knew the business would make it and we'd have sufficient income to get by—except that now the debt load was staggering and the income was all used to pay off that!

In 1992 Inga Vainshtein left a high-pressure, high-reward movie industry job to indulge her love of music by starting a music management company. "I went from earning a six-digit salary with remarkable perks to barely making ends meet," Inga says. But then the second client she signed, a penniless folkie she heard singing in a San Diego coffeehouse, turned out to be Jewel Kilcher, who became a star big enough to be internationally famous by first name only.

As Jewel's manager, Inga says, "I got to travel around the world, experienced the behind-the-scenes of all the awards shows—in other words, got to enjoy my dream." She also made a lot of money—$430,000 in commissions in 1998, the last year she worked with Jewel, according to papers made public as a result of a legal battle that erupted between the two. "Owning your own business," says Inga philosophically, "has its ups and downs."

The days on which the downs seem to be especially sharp for entrepreneurs often coincide with dates significant to the tax collector. Lifestyle entrepreneurs will find themselves dealing with a wide range of tax issues they were sheltered from as employees. If you have always been an employee, odds are you have never been responsible for withholding the required taxes from your paycheck. The money has come out of your pay, to be sure, but your employer has been responsible for figuring the necessary amount, deducting it from your earnings, and cutting the take-home check. At some later date, which varies according to where you are and who you're paying taxes to, the employer has to pay the amount withheld to the tax collector.

In addition to the taxes that are withheld from paychecks, there are often taxes that are paid by employers straight from their own pockets. These are not withheld from employees' wages. For instance, in the United States, 12.4 percent of the wages earned by every employee are withheld for deposit to that employee's Social Security account. (It's more complicated than that in reality—this is the tax code we're talking about, after all—but this approximation will do for our discussion.) But only half that 12.4 percent is actually withheld from the employees' paychecks by employers. The other 6.2 percent is contributed by the employer. So when you are the employer, you have to pay the second half as well. One way to look at this is to consider that you will need to earn about 6 percent more than you did in your old job just to break even on take-home income as a self-employed person.

And there are more taxes. Texas, where I live now, is one of just a handful of states that don't levy their own income taxes. During the years I lived in New York City, there was in addition to the city, state, and federal income taxes, a special income tax levied just on the self-employed citizens of the city. The first time my Texas-born accountant prepared my tax returns for me after I relocated up North, he blurted out in amazement: "They tax you on everything but going to the bathroom up there!"

At one point, I calculated that income, self-employment, and other taxes ate up sixty-two cents of every dollar I earned above a certain amount. This realization had a lot to do with our decision to relocate our family to the more economical environs of Austin. Luckily, the location-independent flexibility of my lifestyle venture made this possible.

If you have employees, the complexity ratchets up. Now you are responsible for withholding federal income, Social Security, and Medicare taxes from your employees' paychecks. You also must withhold their unemployment insurance and other state and local taxes, such as the employee contributions to worker disability and unemployment insurance funds that are mandatory in many states. The paperwork alone can be a significant burden, which is why many small businesses hire out their payroll preparation to a service. You can do it yourself, but it takes time and the penalties for making a mistake can be painful. Once I was a week late mailing in an $11.45 payment for an employee's unemployment insurance tax, and the penalty and interest amounted to $59.88. That kind of thing adds up.

Nor are taxes the only added costs you'll get. For big companies, one of the attractions of having workers who telecommute full-time is that the employer doesn't have to pay to rent or buy office space. Instead, it's the employee who has taken out a thirty-year mortgage on an office to work from. Once you're self-employed, you will be the one paying for a place to house your business, whether it's at home or in commercial space.

Telecommuters are often able to requisition key equipment such as computers and fax machines from their employers. They are also supplied with company letterhead and office supplies, just like other employees. The self-employed person has to buy and maintain a computer and other equipment and purchase all the supplies. Buying a few reams of copy paper and some envelopes probably isn't going to break you. But the time can be a burden too. I spent two full days in one week trying to get my wife's computer working again after the installation of a children's game went awry. At my daily rate, that repair cost more than I'll spend on office supplies in a year.

These outlays in time and money for supplies, maintenance, and required services aren't usually huge sums but, again, they add up. That's especially true in the case of ongoing charges for such items as extra phone lines, internet access, and subscriptions to publications.

Benefits of employment you'll have to do without or provide for on your own include all sorts of other things, from company health plans to paid time off. If doing without them gives you pause, you aren't alone. One of the tough decisions Bill Baker faced when leaving his high-level public relations job to start his own home-based marketing communications business was whether he could get along without the fringe benefits provided by his employer. We're not talking about country club memberships. Bill's concerns were about health insurance and paid vacations and sick days. "It was a real gut-check," Bill recalls, "turning down a salary, vacation, benefits, the whole nine yards, to basically walk across my hallway, sit down in my spare bedroom, and start a business."

Lifestyle entrepreneurship is no panacea. It won't solve all problems or fit all situations. It does a lot, but hardly everything. It won't free you from taking orders from other people. It won't give you total control over your work schedule. It won't allow you to escape the burdensome details of fitting into various systems set up by other people. When it comes to solving lifestyle issues with business tools, the solution does have its limits.

Who's the Boss?

"Being my own boss" or the equivalent probably comes up more often than any other phrase when lifestyle entrepreneurs are describing the motivation and payoff for starting a lifestyle enterprise. But what exactly does it mean? Not long after going into business for yourself, you'll discover that you basically have traded one boss for many bosses. These bosses are your customers. Customers can be both more numerous and just as unreasonably demanding as bosses—if not more so. You may not have realized this in your former position if you were shielded from contact with customers. But "The Customer Is Always Right" is one of those phrases that sounds nice if you're a customer and not particularly bad if you don't have to deal with customers. If you're personally in the business of satisfying customers, however, it can have a distinctly ominous ring.

While I had a few demanding bosses during my days as an employee, none of them were as hard to handle as some of the editors I have had to deal with as a lifestyle entrepreneur. One client routinely returned my articles looking as though they had been through an editorial food processor. The ending would be at the beginning, the beginning at the end, and the middle chopped up and sprinkled throughout, along with scores of questions and half-rewritten sentences ending in ellipses.

The first time this happened, I stared at the heavily marked-up manuscript in shock, wondering if I had been kidding myself about my readiness to solicit business from top-shelf publications. But I dug in and did the work. A couple of weeks after I filed the rewrite, it came back. The ending was at the beginning, the beginning at the end, and the middle had been chopped up and sprinkled throughout. There were slightly fewer ellipses, but overall it appeared as if the editor had never seen the first version. The money wasn't bad, however, the topics suited my background and abilities, and I had learned that most editors became less critical after we had worked together for a while. So I went on to write several more articles for this editor, but with much the same results.

I managed to make things somewhat more palatable after learning that if I waited until the absolute last minute before the magazine had to go to the printer, I could avoid multiple rounds of bare-knuckle, full-contact revision. But it was with a profound sense of relief and even joy when, several months later, a highly experienced and well-respected writer called me up almost frantic with self-doubt and a measure of righteous anger, to ask me whether I'd ever worked with this editor and had my articles kicked back with improbable numbers of questions and requests for rewrites that redefined the term "comprehensive." Our commiserations were salubrious, and we agreed that in the future we'd never work for someone like that again. It's a policy that has served me well, but it was gained at a price in self-confidence and anxiety.

Sometimes, unfortunately, you have little more flexibility in picking your customers than you do your bosses. When the bills are due and you have to make payroll tomorrow, lifestyle concerns recede in importance. You may find yourself having signed a contract to provide services or goods to someone on terms that you would never have chosen except under duress. When that happens, you may find yourself longing for your old, familiar boss.

Last One Out Is the Owner

When you're a fast-track employee, you always leave work ten minutes after the boss, right? But what if you're the owner? The time you leave work, for many owners, is practically never. Michelle Paster truly loves the lifestyle she gets as owner of a tutoring service for students with learning disabilities. But there is a downside that she didn't experience in her former existence as a public school teacher. "What I like about it least is that I'm always doing it," she says. "There are very few times when I take a break from it, because there's always another child to help or another hour to squeeze in. I recently went on vacation and felt much more guilty than I ever did working for someone else. I was counting the number of hours I was missing with kids."

One reason for the extended hours can be that owners are engaged in the same image management game as those ostentatiously hard-working career-building employees. If you've got employees who don't want to leave before the boss, and the boss is determined to set an example, it can add up to some seriously long hours. When you are a one- or two-person company, matters are complicated further by the fact that if you don't do it, it won't get done.

If You Don't Do It, It Won't Get Done

One of the great things about running your own business is that you are responsible for everything. You don't have to check with the higher-ups about taking on a new client, getting rid of an old one, or ordering a new office chair because the padding on the old one is getting thin. On the other hand, that's also one of the worst things. You may sit in that chair until the springs poke holes in your shorts, because you have so many other things to do that you simply never get around to shopping for a new one.

Michelle Paster echoes the entrepreneurs who say that being the boss is the way to go. "If I want to go on vacation, I ask me," Michelle says. But the flip side of that is, no matter what happens, it's her decision and, often, up to her to complete the task at hand. Michelle emphasizes that this one-woman act is her choice. "I want to do things my way," she says. "I feel very strongly that people who are working with kids that have learning difficulties make a tremendous impact in their lives, and I want to be able to control how those kids are impacted."

She feels so strongly about this, in fact, that she sometimes has trouble drawing the line. This is a common issue with entrepreneurs who, in many instances, were primarily motivated by a desire for self-determination when they began their ventures. "I tend to be very controlling in running the business," Michelle confesses. "My highest priority is working with the kids, but I am pretty controlling about the organization and the financial pieces of it. I do try and let other people do things, but I'm not so good at it. But I'm learning. I'm definitely better at it than I was when I started."

Handling Details

The bureaucratic burden for lifestyle entrepreneurs is another detail that is not to be taken lightly. Nearly 20 million people work in civilian jobs for the federal, state, and local governments in the United States, a little over 7 percent of the total population of roughly 275 million.[1] Arrayed against these legions of inspectors, clerks, agents, and others is . . . you. When you are the owner of a small business, everything is up to you. Everything in the way of paperwork, all forms to be filled out, deadlines to be met, bills to be paid, decisions to be made, supplies to be ordered—it all has to come through you.

Small wonder then that government regulation is usually cited as the heaviest burden small business has to bear. In March 2000, at the height of a long-running boom in the business cycle, the fact that small businesses were more concerned about finding employees than about dealing with government regulations was considered significant enough by the Small Business Administration—the U.S. government's agency in charge of handling the interests of small and medium-sized enterprises—that the SBA included the development in a news release. The point is even the government realizes that it's not often that small business owners complain about anything more than they complain about government red tape. [2]

The bureaucratic pressure is relentless. The Internal Revenue Service, as the U.S. government's chief tax-collecting agency, lists twenty-six dates each year that represent various deadlines by which small business owners have to make payments or file various forms. When you add deadlines for states, cities, counties, and other taxing entities—not to mention the requirements of the many regulatory agencies that call for permits to be applied for or renewed, license fees to be paid, and the like—it's clear that you will rarely have much respite between calls for some sort of government-mandated red tape to be dealt with.

Even Michelle Paster's do-everything persona was strained when it came to the accounting end of things. After a year of figuring withholding and filing quarterly payments, Learning Works hired a payroll service to relieve her of that burden. "I had issues about giving up that control," she says. "But when it came time to doing all those tax forms, I found I didn't want to do that."

So there is help available for entrepreneurs whose lifestyles are threatened by red tape. It's not like other people don't have paperwork to slice through. For some lifestyle entrepreneurs, small business ownership actually presents fewer bureaucratic burdens than their previous existences. William H. Hermann retired in 1995 from a forty-five-year career in hospital administration to buy a historic home in Keene, New Hampshire, and turn it into a meeting facility, inn, and conference center. Today Bill crows, "After years of working with committees, boards of directors, government regulations, and large organizational structures, this is freedom!"

The Impact of Failure

The most serious hazard of lifestyle entrepreneurship is not that it won't quite turn out to be what you'd hoped. The gravest danger is that you will go broke. Your outgo will exceed your income over a long enough period that your bills will come to exceed your cash, your liabilities will exceed your assets, your creditors' avarice will exceed their patience, and your venture will become a financial failure. It does happen, and when it does, the impact can be devastating.

I'll take a look at the actual likelihood of financial failure in a few pages. For now, let's just say that failure is not as likely as you may have been given to believe. But the potential impact of business failure is very high, indeed. In the words of Tom Gillis, a veteran small businessman and author of a small business management manual called *Guts & Borrowed Money* (Bard Press, 1997), "Going broke is no fun."

It's not so much that going broke means the end of your dreams of lifestyle business ownership. Going broke can mean several things, and some of them are actually not that bad. If you are unable to pay your bills, you may be able to seek legal protection from your creditors under Chapter 11 of the federal bankruptcy code, keep running your business and, with luck, eventually pay off all or part of the money you owe, emerge from bankruptcy, and be back as a going concern. The actual chances for emerging from Chapter 11, according to a projection by accounting firm PricewaterhouseCoopers, are surprisingly good—about one in three.[3]

Even if that particular business goes under for good, it need not be the end of your career as an entrepreneur. Many notably successful

businesspeople ran early business ventures into the ground before taking flight in later efforts. They include P. T. Barnum, who went bust
before starting "The Greatest Show On Earth"—a lifestyle business if
ever there was one because of the way the entire enterprise reflected
the personal flamboyance of the entrepreneur.

That doesn't sound so bad, right? But bankruptcy is also a public,
painful proceeding in federal court that leaves a permanent record for
anybody to inspect that says you borrowed money and couldn't pay it
back. In its most benign forms, Chapter 11 may be the rosiest scenario.
There's also Chapter 7—involuntary bankruptcy—where your creditors take over your business, break it up, and sell off the pieces with
the connivance of a federal court. There's foreclosure, when a mortgage
holder padlocks the premises after you fail to make the payments, or a
leasing company brings a truck out to repossess and haul off your
equipment when you get too far behind. You can make voluntary
arrangements with creditors, formal or informal, to pay off your bills
by selling off your assets. Or you can simply, quietly, but no less sadly
perhaps, just fade away, paying off everyone out of your own pocket if
necessary and shutting the doors when you're done.

One of the tragedies of business failure is that it usually seriously
depletes the financial resources of the entrepreneur. Could you wind
up with less money than you started with? Sure. I have lost track of
the number of entrepreneurs who have told me that in their industry
the way to make a small fortune is to start with a large fortune. The latest to say this was former obstetrician Dr. Charles Thomas, who was
referring to the Indiana winery he founded and runs in retirement. A
business can take a lot of money to get started and keep going. If the
business is not providing enough money from its operations, it can
deplete the savings of even the most financially secure among us.

As an extreme example of the power of a commercial venture to
consume funds, consider the case of Nelson Bunker and William Her-
bert Hunt. These two Texas oilmen inherited a billion-dollar fortune
from H. L. Hunt, their father and the richest man in the United States
when he died in 1974, but they squandered it in an ill-fated attempt
to corner the world market for silver in the late 1970s. Their losses,

legal fees, and fines from the unsavory venture drove the two billion-aires into corporate and personal bankruptcy. (Don't cry for them, however; as of 2001, Bunker's personal, litigation-proof trust fund, one of six set up by his father to shelter assets transferred to his offspring, still contained more than $200 million.) [4]

In the event that your personal worth doesn't extend to ten figures, loss of your personal savings could be a more significant disaster. Arkansas business professor Don Bradley says he hates to see lifestyle entrepreneurs funded only by barely adequate funds raided from their retirement accounts. "I've see many of them do this and fail and then not have any left for retirement," he warns.

Other risks of successful lifestyle entrepreneurship include embarrassment, damaged personal relationships, and loss of self-confidence. I was concerned about being seen as a failure in the event that free-lance writing did not prove to be a viable enterprise. So I actually started another business at the same time as I quit my job. I began advertising myself as a provider of landscape maintenance services under the name Lawn Ranger. I mowed a few lawns and gathered in a few cash dollars—which came in handy given the long delays in getting paid that most writers experience—and I have fear of embarrassment to thank for it. But things got busy enough on the writing front that before long the Lawn Ranger hung up his clippers for good.

Harm to personal relationships can also occur. It can take a lot of money and a lot of time to start a business, and when that time and money are taken away from a marriage or other relationship, the other people involved may not understand. In *Entrepreneurial Couples* (Davies-Black, 1998), psychologist Kathy Marshack observes, "It is often easier to give up a spouse than to give up one's money." Even if the business succeeds financially, you could wind up with a serious charge against your lifestyle assets if you wind up getting divorced, splitting up with a longtime significant other, or realizing your kids have done a lot of growing up without you.

Your relationship with yourself is another item at risk in lifestyle entrepreneurship. Almost 40 percent of people who closed their small businesses said they probably or definitely wouldn't go into business again, according to a study by the National Federation of Independent Business (NFIB).[5] This loss of confidence in themselves and their abilities might be a good thing if these people were truly not suited to business ownership. But it's hard not to see it as a sort of collateral damage resulting from the impact of failure in a business venture.

The Seven Myths of Small Business Ownership

Small business ownership is not an obscure topic. More than 1,500 U.S. colleges and universities offer some variety of training in entrepreneurship, according to a 2000 count by the Kauffman Center for Entrepreneurial Leadership in Kansas City, Missouri.[6] You would think, by now, that the basic truths about small business ownership would be well established.

But, in my opinion at least, they're not. I count at least seven untruths about small business ownership that have achieved wide circulation despite being incorrect. It might be unfair to call them lies, since they are probably more along the lines of simple misconceptions. Perhaps they should be considered urban legends, since they are so widespread, well-established, and ancient that the source of them can't be determined. But they're not true, and they deserve to be debunked. Some should be corrected because they serve to steer away from entrepreneurship those who probably should consider it. Others make entrepreneurship sound easier than it's likely to be. Still others simply obscure the subject. So let's take a look at them.

We're in the Age of Entrepreneurship

"This is the golden age of entrepreneurship," proclaims a plug for the entrepreneurship program at Mount Royal College.[7] The 10,000-student college in Calgary, Alberta, Canada, isn't alone in considering the period around the year 2000 one of the most fruitful ever in terms of business start-ups. The same term has issued from the mouths and pens of venture capitalists, United Nations educators, business journalists, and even the chairman of the entrepreneurship department of Babson

College in Massachusetts, which is perennially one of the top-ranked small business programs in the United States.

Surely they couldn't be mistaken?

They could. According to D&B, the business information provider formerly known as Dun & Bradstreet, the number of businesses started in the United States fell every year from 1997 to 1999, the latest year for which D&B reported the figures.[8] That was the heart of the period the pundits are talking about when they discuss the so-called entrepreneurial age. And these aren't small declines. Business starts fell to 151,016 in 1999, according to D&B, down 11 percent from 1996.

Other studies tell a similar story. The study by Wells Fargo and the NFIB, referred to earlier in this chapter, found there were more than 4.5 million businesses started in 1998. The number is larger than the one reported by D&B because this study looked at smaller businesses, including those without any employees. But the trend was similar in that the number was down by 600,000 from the year before, part of a decline that began in 1996.[9]

It's likely that the reason this period is so widely viewed as an entrepreneurial eruption is the high profile afforded so many internet start-ups, and the vast financial fortunes reaped by so many of their founders. Mark Cuban, with whom I was acquainted in the 1980s when he was a small business owner in Dallas, in 1995 cofounded Broadcast.com, a provider of video over the internet. Four years later, Mark was worth $2 billion after selling Broadcoast.com to Yahoo. That kind of thing catches your attention. And, as you know if you paid much attention to the sagas of Yahoo!, eBay, and many other dot-com comets, he wasn't the only one to hit it big.

But the fact is, the 1990s experienced no outpouring of entrepreneurs. The most probable reason isn't sinister. It's just that most people found it so easy to get jobs during this period of very low unemployment that they postponed starting businesses. As the economy softens during a typical business cycle, the number of start-ups increases. Other factors also come to bear. One study found a sharp increase in the number of jobless people over age forty who started businesses rather than search for jobs toward the end of 2001. Over the year's first three quarters, the percent of start-ups by forty-plus entre-preneurs rose from 75 percent in the first quarter to 83 percent at midyear and then 94 percent in the third quarter, which ended two and a half weeks after the September 11 terrorist attacks.

The report, by Chicago outplacement firm Challenger, Gray & Christmas, attributed the trend to a combination of age discrimination, a tighter job market, loss of faith in employer-sponsored retirement plans, and a general change in attitude toward work and careers in the wake of the attacks. Company CEO John Challenger was quoted as say-ing, "For many the driving force behind the decision to start a busi-ness may be related to Sept. 11, in that individuals are now committed to living each day to the fullest."[10]

Do What You Love—The Money Will Follow

That is the title of a small business book that is pretty popular, so a lot of people apparently agree with its stated premise. And I wouldn't dis-agree with it entirely. The fact is, you are likely to be more successful when you enjoy your work. However, there is a caveat: Not all things you like to do will make good businesses. I'm all for starting a business that promises to do more than turn a profit. But tuning in to your inner self is not a substitute for some of the more practical planning and analysis methods I'll describe in this book. Following your spirit is not necessarily going to lead to enough money to sustain your body.

Here's Wendy White, continuing the saga of the adventure tour and lodge she opened as a lifestyle venture:

> As the beginning of the fifth year of operation approached this spring, I went back to work as a lawyer. Now, I work five days a week as a lawyer at a third of what I made before I quit practicing; in the evenings I greet guests and take reservations; and on weekends I cook, talk to guests, do the bookkeeping, marketing, and general management. I get a break on Sundays from 12 to 4. Vacations are not possible with a 24/7 business that

needs your personal commitment. However, my consistent income pays for the family needs and the inn operates to pay for itself.

Wendy's sensible advice to would-be lifestyle entrepreneurs is to hang onto their day gig—love it or not—while getting a lifestyle venture underway.

> Start your new business and let it grow first before quitting that job. Find part-time work with an income to get you by. Double all estimates of time and outlay when doing your business planning, and reduce your income projections by at least two-thirds. If you're wrong, great! If you're right, you won't be disappointed and you'll have good planning in place for the future of your business. As a lifestyle choice, operating a small business is not retirement. You'll work longer hours and more days a year than you ever would for someone else. And you will be the last one to get paid— sometimes you won't get paid at all!

None of this is to say a lifestyle venture can't meet your inner and outer needs. There are many examples in this book that show just that. But it's naive to start with the idea that just because you love something it can make a viable business. It makes more sense to start with the idea that you can find something that meets your lifestyle needs and can earn you a living, and then start to look for it.

If You Don't Grow, You'll Die

I confess that in 1990 I wrote an article for *Entrepreneur* magazine that began by recounting the scene from the film *Annie Hall* where Woody Allen explains to girlfriend Diane Keaton his theory that love affairs, like sharks, have to keep moving forward to stay alive. "What we have here," Allen informs Keaton, "is a dead shark." I then commented: "Is your business a dead shark? If it's stopped growing, some would say yes." And next I quoted a small business owner named Jimmy Calano who said, "You must keep growing. Because you're either expanding or you're contracting. You never stay the same."

Live and learn. Ten years later, I was looking at the results of a study of small business owners: 15 percent of them weren't at all interested in growth. This group—one of five culled from the study by pollsters hired by Pitney Bowes Inc.—was dubbed Sustainers. These small business owners often went so far as to declare they didn't want growth and were happy with the way things were. They were also more conservative, less willing to take risks, such as rapid expansion, that could result in the company failing.[11] And, Woody Allen and Jimmy Calano aside, there was no reason to think that they were likely to wind up as shark's bait any sooner than more growth-minded entrepreneurs. You don't have to grow to survive.

You'll Work Harder Than Ever

Starting a business is legendary for requiring a backbreaking amount of work. "Be prepared to work harder and longer than you ever have before"—words from a New Mexico woman who is a small business owner—is a pretty typical warning to would-be entrepreneurs. But that perception isn't necessarily accurate. D&B's 20th annual Small Business Survey of small business owners found that the average owner put in forty-five hours a week. Fourteen percent of them worked fewer than thirty hours per week.[12]

And you can take an even more relaxed approach. Brad Stillahn, who runs a Denver label-printing company called Adstick Custom Labels, has worked hard mainly to make the business capable of running without him. As a result of carefully selecting managers to oversee the twenty-person staff, Brad finds it necessary to put in just twenty hours in a typical week. At a conference for CEOs, Brad decided one colleague was spending too much time at the company. "My recommendation to him was to work forty hours a week, not eighty," Brad recalls. "His recommendation to me was to stop working twenty and start working forty." But given that one of Brad's main goals in starting a business was to be able to limit his hours, that's not likely to happen anytime soon.

You'll Miss That Paycheck

Everybody thinks you're going to miss that weekly slop at the trough of employment—your paycheck. Connecticut home-based marketing consultant Bill Baker said "a drastic cut in pay" from his former job as an account executive was one of his main reservations about taking the plunge into self-employment. Many other lifestyle entrepreneurs mention the salaries they left behind by emphasizing their commitment to satisfying lifestyle needs through business ownership as opposed to fat paychecks. Napa Valley inn owner Larry Grunewald is a typical example. "I left 60,000 stock options and a high-paying job behind," says the former Cisco Systems executive, "but have never regretted it for one moment."

That last qualifier is the key one to keep in mind here. The fact is that while lifestyle entrepreneurs may, from time to time, regret losing their former financial income, few would be willing to trade it for what they are getting now from working with whom they want, traveling when they want, choosing what kind of work they do, living where they want, and working how they want. And not infrequently they actually make more money, in one way or another, so they don't miss their old paycheck at all, even when it's time to pay the bills.

Brad Stillahn was a high-level executive at a billion-dollar company before leaving to pursue his lifestyle venture. He said he initially missed his blue-chip paycheck. But that didn't last forever. "In the last three years, I'm making about twice as much and working only 20 percent as much," he says. "Not bad."

Not bad, indeed. Other entrepreneurs, who are still working harder and bringing home smaller paychecks than they did in their former careers, say other financial rewards help make up for it. Kristin Rhyne laughs grimly when she describes the pay cut she took when leaving the investment banking world to start an airport beauty spa. "It was substantial," says Kristin. But, she adds, now she is the owner of her company rather than an employee. And her finely tuned financial senses say that may pay off more over the long haul. "It's a trade-off," she shrugs. "I'd rather have the equity than the income."

You'll Miss the Security of a Job

"Job security" is one of those phrases that, like "serious fun" and "exact estimate," tries to combine incompatible concepts. The truth is, in general, there is no such thing as a really secure job. The possibility that you could get pink-slipped on any given Friday always exists, no matter how paternal your organization is or how long you've been there. Just ask the former employees of companies with longstanding no-layoff policies, such as IBM and Delta Airlines, who wound up getting laid off. At best, job security is a relative thing. And there's no reason to think that a job—any job—is more secure than owning your own business.

Let's consider the chances that I, for example, am going to be laid off this week. In one sense, the chances are not that bad. In a typical year, about 20 percent of the people I worked for during the previous year stop working with me. Including brand-new customers I didn't work with a year earlier, I lose a client, on average, about once a month. So the chances I'll lose one this week are somewhere around one in four. But am I really insecure?

Not really. Because after I lose that one client, I'll still have a dozen or so left. The chances may be good that a small measure of insecurity will visit me soon. But what are the chances that in one stroke I'll lose all my clients, the equivalent of an employee losing his one and only source of income? The chances are poor. It's never happened, or even come close to happening, and I don't expect it ever will. Add to that the fact that I typically have one to two months' worth of expenses in outstanding invoices, plus a similar or larger amount in backlogged assignments. Also consider that looking for work is something I do almost every day, as opposed to the typical employee who only looks when out of a job. Add it up, and I believe as a lifestyle entrepreneur, my income stream is a lot more secure than it would be were I an employee.

Small Business Is Highly Risky

Everybody knows that small business is extremely risky, similar to playing Russian roulette with your savings and your sanity. Here's what small business author Edward K. Frank has to say on the topic: "It's very disheartening to say the least. Although statistics may vary slightly, most experts contend that 50 percent of small businesses fail within the first year while 80 percent fail within the first five years. What disturbing odds!"[13] It would be pretty disturbing, but in fact those statistics vary more than slightly, and many experts wouldn't touch that 50 percent figure with a 10-foot slide rule.

Karl Vesper, a business professor at the University of Washington and leading expert on new ventures, says these widely disseminated figures are not accurate. Only about 10 percent of new ventures fail each year, according to Vesper's analysis of several such studies. About half of all firms don't make it past the first five years, he adds. But in many fields the survival rates are higher. For instance, 80 percent of high-tech manufacturers make it to their fifth anniversary. "The odds of losing a job in self-employment are probably not much higher than losing in an established firm," he concludes.[14]

Even if things do blow up on you, it may not be the end. The NFIB study found that half of the business owners who closed their companies down said the ventures were profitable over their lifetimes. And 65 percent said they were better off financially—even after terminating their businesses—than they were before starting it.

FOUR

Deciding to Forge Ahead

S ome lifestyle entrepreneurs ease into their ventures so slowly that they hardly realize they are in business until it is already a fact. Others waffle for years or decades before suddenly—and seemingly inexplicably to many of their friends and relatives—flying out of their ruts and into the freedom of lifestyle entrepreneurship. But one thing all lifestyle entrepreneurs have is a point at which a decision was made. At some place and time, a price was put on a product or service, a sale was made, a business plan was written, a loan was taken out, an office rented, a shingle hung, and the dream of lifestyle entrepreneurship became a reality.

The Intuitive Approach

When I was in third grade my grandmother told me, "Marky (she was the only person who ever called me that), you are going to be a writer." I had no idea that she was right. All I knew at the time was that I really liked to read, and I found working with words to be easy and fun. Only later did I realize that she was actually quite wise in her assessment and, as it turned out, correct. Once I came to agree with her, it helped give me the confidence to make some decisions and take some risks.

Maybe that isn't the kind of approach they teach in business school, but lifestyle entrepreneurs don't tend to be spreadsheet jockeys. When it comes time to decide what they're going to do with the rest of their lives, they aren't likely to do a cost-benefit analysis, add up the columns of numbers, and go with whatever Microsoft Excel says they're supposed to do with the rest of their lives. For many, if not most, of them, the decision to start a lifestyle venture, as well as the type of venture to start, begins and ends with a feeling in the gut.

Some of them get their inspiration from actual dreams. Years ago I interviewed a small business owner named Marte Sheeran who said a dream helped push her into entrepreneurship. She was a graduate student at the University of Washington and on track to be a history teacher when she began to have doubts. "It was a very difficult situation for me, trying to figure out what I was going to do," Marte recalled. While away from school on vacation, a series of vivid nighttime dreams jolted her into action. "I was sinking into a bog, going down and down," she said. "There was an enormous sense of being very afraid. That put me in touch with feelings that I was not really happy going into academia."

The dreams helped her clarify her feelings and, after briefly working in a government job, she went back to school and got a business degree. "I had fallen in love with entrepreneurship," she said. "I moved into consulting and then into management with entrepreneurial companies. It was a good decision." Eventually she started a two-person company in Clackamas, Oregon, that published and developed training products for shop floor employees. Looking back on what turned out to be a fulfilling career, Marte said that without the dreams, she might have turned out to be a frustrated history educator. "The dreams released all these emotions and gave me the courage," she said.[1]

Even your horoscope may figure in your decision. Sandy Mayer and her husband, Hank, thought about moving from New York City to Annapolis the first time they visited the historic Maryland city five years ago. Now the owners and operators of the Georgian House Bed and Breakfast, housed in a pre-Revolutionary War home in the city's historic district, Sandy explains how the stars may have impelled her to relocate and start her venture.

"An astrologer in New York told me that I would always be in the home industries," Sandy says. "And I went from clothing design to lodging and food preparation." Whatever the foundation of her rationale, things have worked out fine. "The satisfaction in design and decoration, food presentation, etcetera, is the same," she says, "and Annapolis is a wonderful place to live."

The Intellectual Approach

There is another, more conventional way to decide whether and how to start a business: a more intellectual approach. It has a predictable routine when you're talking about starting conventional types of businesses. Here's how it goes:

1. Start by asking yourself what skills you already possess.
2. Try to match those skills with a business or industry.
3. Read newspaper and magazine articles and talk to people to start researching specific opportunities.
4. Look for emerging trends, unmet needs, ignored niches, and chances to improve on existing products and services.
5. Examine each identified opportunity's "ease of entry," meaning how much money, time, work, and luck it will take to challenge the competition (and there's always some) and overcome the obstacles to make it until you are a going concern.

Now you make a matrix that allows you to numerically score how well your talents and skills fit with identified opportunities, ease of entry, and whatever other characteristics you think are important. Then you add up the numbers and—voila!—the characteristics of your new lifestyle venture will be plainly in view. Researching a lifestyle business opportunity clearly is not like researching other start-up businesses, but some of the same factors come into play.

For instance, you need to make sure your business will satisfy some need in the marketplace. And you need to make sure it can do so profitably—although just how profitably will vary depending on your lifestyle needs. An institutional venture capitalist may demand the likelihood of a 50 percent annual return within four or five years before investing somebody else's money in somebody else's venture. But you may be interested only in earning enough to pay your bills and set aside a little for retirement, gaining the balance of your compensation from the chance to do what you love.

This book is an effort to break new ground in the start-a-business literature, so there's no point in going over the conventional approaches to searching for market opportunities that will support a booming business. Instead, I want to focus your attention and efforts on making sure your lifestyle venture satisfies your lifestyle needs.

Are You Solving the Right Problem?

When it comes to problem solving, no technique works well unless and until you have selected the right problem to solve. One of the most powerful approaches to making sure you are solving the right problem rests on the idea of frames. Frames enclose pictures, help construction workers pour a concrete foundation, and also describe the way we approach a problem. Framing in a decision-making sense is eloquently described in *Winning Decisions: Getting It Right the First Time* (Doubleday Currency, 2001), a book by J. Edward Russo and Paul J. H. Schoemaker. These two decision-making experts describe frames as ways of looking at the world. The frame through which you see the world limits what you see and controls what you focus on, so they clearly have a major effect on your decisions. They are hard to see themselves, however, and so are often hard to change.

When it comes to making a decision about lifestyle entrepreneurship, you often have to change the frame through which you view the world of business. In an important sense, this book's basic aim is to change the way people see business, so that they can view it largely or even primarily as a means to satisfy their nonfinancial needs in addition to putting money in their pockets. I went through a frame shift on this topic myself in the last few years.

When I first got out of college, my goal was to be a famous investigative reporter like Bob Woodward and Carl Bernstein, the journalistic icons for many young people in the 1970s. After I graduated in 1981, I went to work as a police reporter for a small Southern newspaper, a first career step also taken by David Halberstam, another famous journalist of the era. To say that I had no interest in business journalism at that point would have been a major understatement. I barely realized that such a vocation existed.

But after a while, I came to recognize that it was a long way from the police beat on the *Beaumont Journal* to head of the Capitol bureau for The *Washington Post*. I didn't have an Ivy League education and connections like Halberstam, and I couldn't realistically expect to be lucky enough to stumble onto a Watergate-sized story as Woodward and Bernstein had. Furthermore, I didn't have the fire in the belly to pursue public affairs journalism as some of my more zealous and ideological colleagues did.

Business journalism at the time was just beginning to boom, with many daily newspapers publishing separate business sections for the first time. It seemed there was a lot of opportunity there, and when I got a job offer to work for a prosperous business weekly in Houston, I took it. But I soon began to have trouble with the work. I couldn't figure out what made a business story newsworthy. Why was one press release worthy of front-page coverage, while another inside tip was deemed uninteresting?

Then one day it clicked: In public affairs journalism, if anybody made a financial profit on anything, it was a sin, and that made it news. If a county commissioner had passed out a road-paving contract to a crony who then paved the commissioner's driveway for free, that was definitely news. In business writing, on the other hand, the situation was reversed: If anybody didn't make a profit, that was a sin and that was news. If an oil well drilling company overpaid when it bought another drilling company and the shareholders lost money, that was news. There were wrinkles, of course. It depended on how much money was lost, and in some cases an unusual profit was also news. Of course, if the company was big and important enough, news of either profit or loss would have to be reported. But the essential change in frame had taken place. I knew what was business news and what wasn't, and I was ready to embark on the career that has proven so interesting and liberating.

How can you make sure the frame through which you're viewing lifestyle entrepreneurship will help you make a good decision? There are three major steps.

Be Aware That Your Frame Exists

Try to identify the parameters of the frame you are using. Ask yourself, How am I viewing this problem? Also consider the frames your advisors and significant others are using. When you compare the way they and you see the issue, you will probably become aware of frames. Sometimes these frames other people use can be liberating. Craft businesswoman Cheryl Fey got interested in decorating her home with stencils and helped several friends embellish their own homes, but she needed another person's frame to see it as a business opportunity. "It was my husband, Dave, who encouraged me to take my part-time stenciling of friends' homes and turn it into a full-time business," says Cheryl. "I had never really taken my art seriously. After all, I had a degree in chemistry! Knowing that I needed to expand my offerings, I spent one summer creating a large portfolio and enlarging the parameters of stenciling. My first job was in September, and by December I was booked until the following June. It has never stopped since then, and that was fifteen years ago. I have been a full-time artist ever since."

See If the Frame You're Using Fits Your Needs

Are you seeing lifestyle entrepreneurship in a way that limits your options? For instance, are you hating your job and seeing no way out of it? Do you find work activities you once enjoyed, such as business travel, now unspeakably onerous? This is a common symptom of bad frame fit. That was one of the things motivating Madison Avenue ad-executive-turned-Main-Street-bookstore-owner Maryalice Hurst. "I didn't want to live like I did when I was thirty any longer," Maryalice says of her decision to leave New York City for Conway, Arkansas. "I once thought traveling in planes was very glamorous. But I didn't want to do that any more."

Modify Your Frame or Build a New One

This is the payoff step and it's not always easy to do, but the main problem in changing frames is realizing that they even exist. By this point, you're already aware of the way you're framing the problem. Even when you know what your frame is, it can still be difficult to change. But, again, the fact that you're even reading this book means you have already sensed a shift in the way you view business ownership's potential to fill your lifestyle needs.

Shifting frames is almost a universal experience for lifestyle entrepreneurs. Having been raised to consider business ownership as a purely or mostly financial gambit, these entrepreneurs have had to change their viewpoints to even consider owning a business for other purposes. Lera Chitwood's decision to quit her high-paying job and buy a country inn in Dillsboro, North Carolina, was reframed by a combination of events including divorce, her son leaving for college, her job heading into a dead end, and a bout with cancer. "For the first time in my life, I wanted to work in the home," Lera says of her reframing experience. "I had never thought of running a B&B, but now it seemed to fit."

This sort of reframing due to a confluence of external forces is common for lifestyle entrepreneurs. If you feel you need to reframe the way you look at business ownership, there are several approaches the *Winning Decisions* authors recommend that have been used by lifestyle entrepreneurs I have interviewed. You can start by looking for somebody else's frame that could fit your needs, perhaps with some alterations.

For instance, ownership of a bed-and-breakfast is one popular lifestyle entrepreneurship solution. What kind of frame do B&B owners use? Would it fit yours? The frame most of them use is to see lifestyle entrepreneurship as consisting of a business that lets them live in an attractive location, meet lots of interesting people, and work in the same place they live. Is that a frame you can use? Be aware of its limitations: B&B owners rarely work short hours, and they're always on duty on holidays and weekends. Their business isn't as flexible as it could be either. Once you own a B&B, you won't find it easy to pull up stakes and move somewhere else. You may want to consider other frames, like the one used by home-based knowledge workers such as marketing consultants.

Another way to shift your frame is to talk it over with people whose opinions you respect. Other people often use different frames. You can pick and choose elements of your frames until you come up with the one that you need. Sometimes, it should be noted, outsiders' frames will be narrower, less accurate, or worse in some other way than the one you're already using. Carol Edmondson gave up a high-paying, high-tech, big-city job with one of the world's largest companies to move to Cape Cod and ply her cooking and entertaining skills as owner of the Captain Freeman Inn in Brewster, Massachusetts. When she announced her plans, the news was poorly received almost everywhere. But she didn't buy into that frame. "Contrary to all the advice I got, this was the absolutely right decision for me," she says, ten years after making the move. "I have become a firm believer in going with your gut, even when it's not the popular route."

Bottom line on framing your decision: Know your frame is there, how it limits you, and what you can do to change it if necessary.

Gathering Information

Once you're sure you're solving the right problem, it's time to gather information. Again, this is a topic heavily covered in business-starting manuals. To summarize, here are the places you should go to find information about business opportunities:

- Business publications. Read the *Wall Street Journal, Business-Week, Entrepreneur,* and other general business publications to learn about the United States and world economy, business trends, and opportunities. For a less U.S.-centric look, try *The Economist* or *Financial Times*. Country- and region-specific business publications include Canada's *Financial Post* and the *Far Eastern Economic Review* serving Asia. Also read the industry-specific magazines known as trade journals that cover the field you are interested in. One of the best examples of this is *Advertising Age*, the Bible of the ad industry. Once you've decided on a geographic location for your business, focus some of your reading on local business and general-interest publications.

- Government sources. In the United States, the Small Business Administration, a branch of the U.S. Department of Commerce, is a good place to start looking for information about industries, trade opportunities, and business activities. Many other federal agencies, from the Bureau of the Census (also part of the Commerce Department) to the Bureau of Labor Statistics (part of the Department of Labor), collect and disseminate information that entrepreneurs are likely to find both very useful and unobtainable elsewhere. You don't have to be an American entrepreneur to use and profit from these resources, by the way. The Commerce Department has troves of data on trade with many countries of the world, much of it available to anyone for the asking, including citizens of other nations. Globally, the Organization for Economic Cooperation and Development maintains a great deal of publicly available information on trade, economies, and related topics on its thirty member countries as well as scores of other nations. There are local equivalents in many other countries. In the United Kingdom, for instance, there is the Small Business Service, an agency of the Department of Trade and Industry that provides information and advice for business owners.
- Industry associations. These range from the general, such as the Chamber of Commerce (chapters of which exist in most cities around the world), to the specific. Pick a niche, any niche—from the one occupied by the Aluminum Association of Washington, D.C., and its 200 members (such as Alcoa) to the Zero Balancing Association, a somewhat less-prominent organization of mind-

body healers in Charlottesville, Virginia. You can get some good information from these groups, including market size statistics, numbers of competitors, how-tos, safety tips, information on government regulation, and early looks at upcoming legislation.

- Personal contacts. Many businesses have been started because someone came up to someone at a party and said, "You know what? I can never find what I need to...," and went on to describe a market opportunity that somehow was slipping beneath the radar screens of the sophisticated market researchers at the big companies. When people tell you they're frustrated because of an unmet need, or thrilled by the appearance of some oddball product or service, or amazed that you haven't tried to make a business out of some hobby you pursue, listen to them. Take it with a grain of salt, but don't throw it away. Sometimes, let it be said, you have to ignore personal input. Stephanie Turk would never have started her Pasadena, California, company to create fancy lingerie for full-busted women if she'd listened to her mom. "My mother thinks I'm crazy," says Stephanie, who ended a fifteen-year career as a civil engineer in order to design bras.

- Yourself. Lifestyle entrepreneurship is about your life, so it's appropriate when the inspiration for the business you start comes from your own needs that aren't being met by the market. Business history is replete with examples of people who started businesses to provide products or services that few people other than themselves recognized as being of value. Stephanie Turk is one of those people. Maybe the most famous are Steve Jobs and Stephen Wozniak, who thought it would be really great if you could buy a small computer for personal use. Very few people outside the members of the Homebrew Computer Club, a Silicon Valley hobbyist group, agreed with them. Yet that was the beginning of Apple Computer.

But it's just as important, when looking into a business, that you gain information about how it will satisfy the lifestyle needs you have in mind as well as whether it will prove a commercial success. How do you go about doing that? Probably the best way is to try it out. Work in the field you have chosen for your venture for a period of time before quitting your job and going out on your own. Many entrepreneurs, including myself, have done this successfully. It allows you to gain almost as much experience as you would working full-time at your venture, while avoiding the lost income and emotional stress of trying to make a living out of it from the get-go.

Erin Allen had eighteen years of experience as a court reporter and an entirely incompatible yearning to become a beachside innkeeper. What to do? She and her husband purchased a dilapidated Lake Worth, Florida, lodge and started working on the long list of things that would have to be done to transform it into the beautiful Mango Inn. Renovations alone took a long time, and it took even longer to learn enough about the business and build the customer base large enough so she could devote herself to it exclusively. "I worked simultaneously as a full-time court reporter and innkeeper for three and a half years until the inn was doing well enough that I was finally able to become a full-time innkeeper only and leave behind my prior career," Erin says.

Brad Stillahn, the hardly working Denver printer, kept his corporate job for four years after buying his business. Moonlighting as a lifestyle entrepreneur helped him learn the industry, reinvest profits in building the company, and still insulate his family's finances from the cash needs of a young business. I did something similar by freelancing part-time for five years before quitting my job to freelance full-time. This part-time approach is an eminently sensible and effective method for learning about an industry prior to entering it full-time as a lifestyle entrepreneur.

Don't have the time to work part-time at a lifestyle venture for research purposes? Take a sabbatical or leave of absence. About one in four large companies now have formal sabbatical policies. Most people taking sabbaticals spend their time traveling, writing, volunteering, renovating homes, or learning to play a musical instrument, according to a vice president of human resources for one big company that offers paid leaves. However, it's also common for burned-out corporate workers to spend their time away from work crafting a business plan designed to make the separation permanent.

If you can't get a paid sabbatical at your corporate job, consider taking one without pay, even quitting your job if necessary, to spend time mulling over your options and researching opportunities before actually starting your business. After leaving his job with a training firm, Tim Smith spent time in a monastery in Nepal reflecting on his life and aims. When he left the monks, he started his own leadership consulting firm, Wheelwright Associates of Carmel, California. "This was my own way of deepening my understanding of what I do," Tim explains. "I spent some time really clarifying for myself what I wanted my practice to be, who I wanted to work with, and what I wanted the outcomes to be, not only for myself but for other people as well." [2]

You may even be able to get your employer to pay you to leave and start your lifestyle venture. Darcy Volden Miller had already decided to quit her job with a large electronics company to explore working at home so she could be with her infant son. At about the same time, her employer started trying to shrink the workforce and began offering handsome payouts to anybody who would voluntarily separate. "I was probably the first person to throw my hand up," Darcy says. "The money Motorola was offering would give me a chance to try it out for a year and give me a year with my baby."

Darcy actually spent that time with two babies. In addition to diapering and feeding little Landen, she had conceived an on-line business retailing baby gifts and mothering-related items, called Littledidiknow.com. Three years later, Darcy's venture was bringing in more than her husband's full-time work. And she was still doing it from home with little Landen, as I can testify from hearing him hollering in the background as I tried to interview her over the phone from her home in Austin.

Taking a New Job

You don't have to quit your current job or even take another one part-time to explore a lifestyle venture. You can take a whole new job with the plan of learning enough about an industry or opportunity to increase your odds of making a go of it later on.

That was the strategy taken by Rich Owen and Todd Wichmann, then a pair of chemical engineers working at Procter & Gamble, who decided to pursue assignments in other areas of the company. Rich wound up going through sales and then finance, while Todd toured marketing, product development, and brand management. All the while, they were kicking around the idea of someday having their own company, probably a regional detergent maker that sold private-label brands to grocery stories. But when Procter & Gamble announced it was selling off the old but neglected Oxydol brand of laundry detergent, they saw their chance to go national with a brand that had lots of untapped potential. They left P&G, started Redox Brands, Inc. in West Chester, Ohio, and raised enough money from investors to purchase Oxydol from its parent.

Eighteen months later the co-CEOs had tripled sales of the venerable product and were on a track to record a mind-bending $70 million in annual sales. What made it possible was savvy application of the array of skills they had learned while on their former employer's payroll. "We were in a unique position to exploit a deal like this," says Rich.[3]

Making the Decision

In a sense, I made the decision to become self-employed in a college journalism class. That was the first time I was exposed to the idea of freelance writing as an actual career path. But between that time and the date I actually made the dream come true was a period of several years, many false starts, and a lot of wonder and worry. Fortunately, that's not the only way you can come to a decision about pursuing the entrepreneurial lifestyle. Many people report the decision arrives in a flash; others grow into it slowly. Some can tell you the precise moment they booked their first sale or took out their business license. Others say it happened without them even noticing it.

For Stephanie Turk, it was a combination of everything. One day at her job as an engineer with the California state transportation department, something snapped. Time and again, her suggestions and ideas had been smothered by the bureaucracy. "Working with government, it's easy to get frustrated," she says. "You have ideas and want to do different things, but there's red tape." Eventually, Stephanie decided to try something completely different.

Her solution started with attending business school at UCLA while continuing to work part-time at her job. She used accumulated sick leave and vacation time to keep earning a full-time salary while earning her MBA. She still wasn't thinking about entrepreneurship, however. Instead, she planned to get some kind of information technology job after graduation. But while at UCLA, she took a class on entrepreneurship. "One of our assignments was to write a feasibility study," Stephanie says. "When I was looking for a topic, I thought about how frustrated I was finding lingerie for myself. I looked into it and the more I looked into it, the more feasible it sounded."

She started looking for patterns, fabric sources, cutting houses, and sewing contractors. She thought of a name, WearUnder. She got a Small Business Administration–guaranteed loan to created her first production run. "Three years later," she says, "here I am."

Removing Roadblocks

For many would-be lifestyle entrepreneurs, the way is blocked by obstacles. That was my story. I knew I wanted to be a lifestyle businessman for five years before I cut the strings and did it full-time. During that time, the obstacles in my way included: doubt about whether I could earn a living freelancing, difficulty in refinancing my home loan so the mortgage payment would be affordable, and reluctance to have surgery done while I was covered by my employer-sponsored health plan. Achieving my revenue goals was probably the stickiest problem. While the others yielded to a focused attack—I finally found a mortgage company that would approve my refinancing application and gritted my teeth and had the surgery—the income issue resolved itself gradually and almost without my noticing. One day while preparing my annual federal income tax return, I realized my self-employment income from the prior year totaled almost a third of what I made from my regular job. I'd brought in about $9,000 from the business and was earning $27,700 in salary. The key was realizing that I made that much usually working only Tuesday nights and Saturday mornings. It was ten or twelve hours a week tops. If I could make a third of my salary only working part-time at freelancing, I realized, I could very likely make at least as much if I worked at it full-time. This was the trigger that set me off.

Since then, I've talked to many people who waited until their part-time lifestyle business income reached a certain percentage of their employee wages. That percentage varies widely, from 100 percent to 10 percent. I believe 30 percent is a good rule of thumb, partly because it worked for me and partly because it worked for others. It all depends, too, on how many hours you're working in your lifestyle venture while still employed. If you're working two full-time schedules and one of them is only bringing in half as much money, that's not too encouraging.

Family issues are also often cited as entrepreneurial roadblocks. Many entrepreneurs wait until they have had children, until those children have reached school age, or even until those children have left the house for good before starting their lifestyle ventures. There's not much you can do about that, other than keeping the faith and staying patient and focused. Children only grow up so fast. But if the obstacle is a partner or other family member who is concerned that your venture will consume too much of your time, the family's finances, or some other precious resource, you can with luck explain to them how important this is to you and what you're doing to minimize the risk and the impact on the family.

The toughest family nut to crack is when your significant other is blocking the way. It's not hard to understand why a spouse or partner might not want you take a lifestyle venture flyer. They may have heard stories about long hours, lost wages, and heavy debts associated with small business ownership. They may also have other motivations. For instance, jealousy. Darcy Volden Miller says the success of her on-line baby gifts venture, Littledidiknow.com, is beginning to eclipse her husband's earnings from his business, and she feels it's causing a strain. "I've become more successful with my business and kind of outgrown his business," Darcy says. "Maybe it's the male ego thing, that the woman is making more than he is, but I sense there's something there."

Azriela Jaffe, in her book *Honey, I Want to Start My Own Business* (HarperBusiness, 1997), has two main recommendations for would-be entrepreneurs whose spouses are standing in the way.

First, she says, appreciate your spouse's sacrifice. You may feel as though this is your baby all the way, but remember: Your spouse is going to have to do the dishes when you are on the phone with customers; the house you plan to pledge as collateral for start-up capital is half-owned by your other half; and those kids will have to be brought up by someone while you are closeted with suppliers, lenders, employees, and whoever else comes along. Realizing this up front will help your spouse bend to let you get what you want.

Second, be as flexible as you can. If you never have believed in wasting money on liability insurance premiums but fears of a damages lawsuit is keeping your spouse awake, then offer to call the agent and cut the check yourself. You're asking someone to give up something important—namely, you, to a considerable degree—so be ready to give up something in return. Being flexible also means being willing to compromise, whether that involves delaying your lifestyle start-up for a while until some other objective has been reached (such as paying off the house) or keeping your current job while you try out lifestyle entrepreneurship on the side.

Whatever the issue, you need to talk about it and reach a joint decision, stresses Anne Warfield, who runs a home-based Minneapolis communications consulting firm Impression Management Professionals with her husband, Paul Cummings. "You have to be realistic about what you want and need," says Anne.

And never forget that spouses can be allies instead of obstacles to lifestyle entrepreneurship. *Entrepreneurial Couples* author Kathy Marshack identifies several different types of successful entrepreneurial couples, including solo entrepreneurs who have supportive spouses, dual entrepreneurs who have separate businesses, and so-called copreneurs who labor alongside each other in the same venture. Anne Warfield says Impression Management Professionals has, by design, been a tool for she and her husband to come together rather than a wedge to drive them apart. "We were doing a lot of traveling and too much work," she says of their pre-entrepreneurship lives. "We didn't want to miss the kids' plays and give up time together. We realized we needed to be doing something together."

The Electric Moment

Once you have opened your mind to the possibility of lifestyle entrepreneurship, it may only be a matter of time. You may be in the middle of working at a business you simply wandered into almost by accident, or you may just be taking a shower and getting ready to go to your job—but the thought will strike you with the clarity of a lightning bolt. At that moment, you'll know what it is that you want to do. It happened to Susan Martin just that way. "I was on the phone with a good friend of mind," says Susan, a Brooklyn resident who quit a garment industry career to become a personal career coach. She had recently had a baby and was anguishing over how to reconcile the impossible demands of working in a hotly competitive field, sustaining a marriage, and parenting her young child. "My friend said, 'How in the world are you going to find out what you want to do when you're under the kind of pressure you are?'"

It was a simple question, veiling a suggestion that she step back from her job and take a break before doing something else. And it was one she'd been hearing for some time from other friends, her husband, and a therapist. But this time it hit like a hammer. "For some reason, I was ready to hear it," Susan says. "And that was the moment. I realized this was what I wanted to do."

PART TWO

Taking the Plunge

FIVE

Selecting an Option

General Electric is a business, and the kid down the street who adorns your front door with flyers advertising his car-washing service has a businesses too. Probably, however, neither of these businesses is right for your lifestyle. Somewhere in between? Somewhere around? Somewhere different? The answers are yes, yes, and yes. The world is awash with varieties of businesses, from one-person, home-based consulting firms to multinational industrial conglomerates. And there are more varieties being discovered all the time.

Some of the new ones are high profile spin-offs of widely recognized changes in our economy and society. Take Darcy Volden Miller. Ten years ago, who would have dreamed a company could be built on the idea of using a global public computer network to cooperatively market baby gifts and related items, created by work-at-home moms? Yet Littledidiknow.com is an eminently viable business, both in terms of filling Darcy's need to stay home with her young son and providing income. In fact, says Darcy, "It's done exponentially better than I could ever have dreamed of."

Other innovations seem to have grown from some strange place in our society that few ever think about. Patti Glick has worked since 1996 as The Foot Nurse, giving lunchtime seminars on foot health, screenings, foot measurements, and shoe-fitting tips to employees of companies in the San Francisco Bay Area. How much demand could there be for that kind of service? So much that Patti has enough business to fill a full workweek, despite doubling her price from $150 to $300 per brown-bag seminar. "If you just want the presentation, that's $300," she clarifies. "If you want the foot measurement, that's another $300."

In addition to being full of different kinds of businesses, the entrepreneurial plane is crowded with techniques, strategies, and systems for selecting the right business. Look around just a little bit and you'll be overrun with checklists, cost-benefit analyses, spreadsheets, and other highly objective-looking tools for picking the proper business for you to invest your time and money in.

Unfortunately, none of these approaches pays adequate attention to the component we're paying the most attention to—namely, lifestyle. Lifestyle doesn't lend itself to analysis. Lifestyle decisions don't always result from weighing the pros and cons. Like Debbie Gisonni, a Redwood City, California, workshop leader, motivational speaker, and author whose decision to leave her job as a technology magazine publisher was pure reaction.

"I just left," Debbie says of her 1998 decision. "I didn't know what exactly I was going to do. I just had a few ideas about projects." She wrote a book called *Vita's Will* (Writer's Club Press, 2000) that talked about what she'd learned when four family members died in rapid succession. "A business spawned from that," she says, somewhat enigmatically. This is not the kind of strategy that excites approval from a professor of entrepreneurship. But these are the decision processes that often lead to lifestyle businesses.

Whether you decide with a calculator or a dartboard, your main options for business ownership remain much the same: You can either start a new business from scratch, buy an existing business, or do something in between.

Starting a Business

The person who starts a business is the classic entrepreneur who begins with nothing but an idea and somehow creates an organization that takes in money, materials, and effort and satisfies customers while sustaining itself. There's something magical about that, and magic is, at bottom, what lifestyle entrepreneurship is all about.

If you're starting fresh, a couple of the main options are to freelance, working from home in a one-person, low-overhead operation, or to moonlight, sticking with your current job for a while and working at your new venture evenings and weekends. For business-buyers, the options are buying a one-of-a-kind operation or buying into a franchise, which I consider more like buying a business than starting one since you're joining an existing system.

Let's talk first about straight-up starting a business. The most basic description of a business opportunity, according to University of Washington entrepreneurship expert Karl Vesper, is that it is a chance to obtain a profit from the difference between benefits and costs. I like the way Karl avoided using the term "revenues" instead of "benefits." As lifestyle entrepreneurs know, not all benefits come adorned with dollar signs.

Hugh Daniels has owned and operated the Old Miner's Inn in Park City, Utah, for eighteen years without ever showing a cent of after-tax net income. The inn does generate a modest $15,000 to $18,000 a year in operating profit, which is the difference between what he takes in and what it costs to run the inn and pay the mortgage, utilities, suppliers, and employees. But that turns into a loss after taking into account the effects of depreciation. Depreciation is a paper loss that is called for by accounting rules. It reflects the supposed year-to-year decrease in value of assets, in this case the Old Miner's Inn itself. Such a paper loss can be a good thing for people like Hugh because it allows them to reduce their tax burden and even shelter part of their income from taxes. Unfortunately, tax laws limit the number of years you can continue to depreciate an asset, as well as the total amount you can write off as a charge against depreciation. Muses Hugh, "When the depreciation's used up, we'd be in serious trouble."

Hugh is not in serious trouble now, however, nor has his business failed to deliver serious "benefits" for the last eighteen years. "We've never paid for a place to live," he notes. "It's paid for our food, our health insurance, our car, and our furniture. Am I getting $100,000 a year? No. But just in stuff that most people would have to pay for like utilities and mortgage, it's actually a pretty good salary. And it's not taxable, which is kind of nice.

"The other thing you get is your lifestyle," adds Hugh, who moved to the tiny, high-altitude ski area from Southern California. "We live in a mountain resort that's gorgeous."

Taxes and accounting aside, when a business starts, it is almost miraculous. It is sort of like whipping up a hurricane with a box fan. You take an idea, apply some money and more work, and you create a system that takes in money for products and services other people want, sends some back to suppliers and lenders and employees, and, if all goes well, keeps enough of a surplus to repay the person who originated the idea in the first place. But it's only sort of like a miracle. People have studied and analyzed what it takes to make a good start-up endlessly. A lot of it depends on what's going on around you. Here are some of the agreed-upon scenarios when an idea may be good enough to start a business:

- Technological shifts, especially driven by proprietary technology you have discovered or obtained the right to use. Lonnie G. Paulson invented the Super Soaker water pistol in his bathroom and today receives an estimated $10 million annually in licensing fees.
- A shift in population demography, market tastes, or consumer lifestyles that create unmet market demand you know how to satisfy. Ron Kipp realized that sport scuba diving was in its infancy and was poised for rapid growth, which allowed his Grand Cayman lifestyle entrepreneurship business to grow along with it.
- Regulatory shifts. There is a trend among American states to offer to dismiss a traffic ticket from a driver's record upon completion of an approved defensive driving course. As this trend has grown, so have the number and diversity of driver training schools. Currently, there are twenty-eight states on the bandwagon and innumerable driver schools offering courses by video, over the Internet, and even presented by a stand-up comic.

- Economic events. The boom in prosperity fueled by rising stock prices in the 1990s created countless opportunities for financial advisors, stock tip letter publishers, brokers, and others.
- For a lifestyle entrepreneur, we would add: Personal events. Changes in circumstances, ranging from loss of a job to mid-career burnout, while not being sufficient in themselves to produce a winning business, can provide adequate motivation to find or create one.

After watching the excesses of the millennial dot-com investing frenzy, I hesitate to state that it takes more than a hospitable environment to create a business. When people can raise tens of millions of dollars for a business plan that calls for selling sofas on-line, it's hard to rule anything out. But in fact, a high percentage of these wacky-sounding dot-com businesses turned out not to be viable. So what are the characteristics of a good idea under normal circumstances? Again, there is some agreement on these.

- You have something better than the competition. The value difference has to be enough that you can charge enough to make a profit and still win customers.
- You have or can get the money required to fund the start-up, and you possess or know who can provide the technical competence, business know-how, and other resources it will take.
- You will get adequate lifestyle benefits out of the business to make it worthwhile.

I'll go into this last item on lifestyle paybacks in much more detail. For now, let's just say that the potential benefits will be such things as being able to work

- in the place you want,
- with the people you want,
- for the hours you want,
- doing the kind of work you want,

- with the flexibility you want, and
- ideally, with enough freedom to change things around more should your lifestyle needs change.

Starting a business from scratch may be mysterious in some ways, but has some very down-to-earth built-in benefits. One of the most important is that you can often get by with a much smaller initial investment when you are starting a business as opposed to buying one. When you buy an existing business, you have to pay at once for the value that has been built up by the previous owner, perhaps over a period of many years. When you start a business, you can start small and build your way up. So if your financial resources are limited, starting a business may be your only option. It's not necessarily a bad one. Remember, Michael Dell started off selling computers he assembled in his dorm room and became the world's largest personal computer maker.

Some other benefits of making a clean start include:

- A high degree of control. You're making the rules, not following somebody else's.
- A great deal of flexibility. If the goal changes, you can change the company.
- The fun of creation. For many years, it seemed almost magical to me that I could come up with an idea for an article or book, find a publisher who would agree to publish it, and get a check in the mail.

With all these benefits, it's small wonder that two out of three business starts are new ventures. But maybe these people haven't looked at the downside of starting a new venture compared to buying an existing business, such as:

- Higher risk. When you're going where no lifestyle entrepreneur has gone before, even if your frontier is just being the first home-based medical claims analysis service in that part of the state, there's more risk than stepping into an already-running system.

- More work. One of the reasons you can start a business for less cash than you can buy one for is that you can substitute sweat equity—or your own unpaid labor—for purchase money. That's good, and it's bad.

Taking the bad with the good, starting a new venture makes a great deal of sense for most lifestyle entrepreneurs. However, lifestyle entrepreneurs tend to be—although not all are—middle-career types with resources adequate to doing more than bootstrap a minimal start-up. These experienced workers often have the ability to manage a larger, already up-and-running enterprise; at the same time, they may not have the fire in the belly to work long hours creating sweat equity. For those reasons, buying a business is another idea to consider.

Buying a Business

One-third of the people who want to get into business do it by buying an existing concern. While buying a business lacks some of the intrinsic romance of the entrepreneur who creates an enterprise out of nothing, that doesn't mean it has to completely lack charm. When Ron Kipp jumped IBM's ship to run a scuba diving business in the Caribbean, he bought an existing operation rather than try to create one from scratch. Bob Soto's Diving Ltd. was the oldest diving company in the world when Kipp took it over in 1981. That gave it nearly unmatched name recognition in an industry that was fast-growing and still so new that few consumers had any loyalty at all. "His operation was pretty crummy," Ron recalls, "but I had stars in my eyes." He was able to swing an advantageous purchase arrangement with the retiring owner and felt sure that fresh enthusiasm and an old name would add up to a successful lifestyle business.

If you'd like to emulate Ron's success, there are three steps to buying a business that will help you.

1. Find the industry you want to be in and the company that you want to purchase.

2. Analyze and evaluate the company to see how much it's worth.

3. Negotiate the deal.

Ron's approach to the first step was to start with two facts about recreational scuba diving in 1981. First, he really liked it. Second, a growing number of other people did too. Being IBM-trained as a business manager, he didn't just stop there.

"I started to do due diligence on it," Ron says. On his frequent sport diving trips around the Caribbean and elsewhere, he would talk to divers and dive shop owners. "I found out there was a tremendous amateur aspect to it. A lot of the people who were in the dive shops and resorts were just there because they liked to dive. They weren't businesspeople. I thought I'd have an edge because while I liked to dive, I knew you have to have a good business case or it'll crumple around you."

Once diving was certified as the industry, the question was: Where? He checked out the Florida Keys, Cozumel in Mexico, and Bonaire in the Netherlands Antilles, among others. Everywhere he found problems: Florida wasn't tropical enough, Mexico required Spanish fluency, and so forth. "Then I came to Grand Cayman and it just all hit," Ron says. Bob Soto, the company's founder, was burned out and ready to sell. Ron decided that, if the company checked out, this was where he would try to buy.

The second step was to analyze his prospect in detail. That wasn't all that difficult. The main assets were three boats tricked out for diving expeditions. Ron ran the numbers cocktail napkin–style to come up with an annual sales projection. "You take a dive boat and put twenty people on it at $50 and multiply it times 365," he explains.

So far so good, but Ron kept scrutinizing Soto's operation. The boats, he found, were not in good repair, and the business wasn't much better. But he saw another asset that seemed to contain appreciable value. "I'd get a five-year lease at the Holiday Inn, which in 1980 was the only game in town," he said. "I saw the people walking around the hotel just starved for things to do and this beautiful ocean just sitting out there—and this dive shop."

Ron eventually arrived at a decision to buy the business and began the third phase: negotiating the deal. Soto agreed to a purchase price of approximately $500,000, with $200,000 down and the balance to be paid over seven years. Ron put up half the down payment from personal savings and family loans and borrowed the rest from Cayman National Bank. "It worked," he says, twenty years later. In fact, he paid off the seven-year loan from Soto in three years.

Other business buyers also report that purchasing an existing concern can save time, reduce risk, and simplify financing; often, the current owner will finance the purchase, as Soto did for Ron. On the downside, it requires a large capital outlay up front to purchase a going concern. You can start very small with a new business, on the other hand, and increase your investment gradually. It's also hard to know precisely what you're buying until you've bought it. And, in the case of a business that hasn't satisfied customers well, its history can limit rather than leverage you.

Franchise Facts

No discussion of business ownership options would be complete without a mention of franchises and business opportunities. Some lifestyle entrepreneurs would prefer, however, that any such mention be dismissive. Jane Pollak may in some ways be the prototypical lifestyle entrepreneur because of the quirky nature of her business, her success (she has sold hand-decorated eggs for more than thirty years and earns a six-figure income), and the fact that she has written a book called *Soul Proprietor: 101 Lessons from a Lifestyle Entrepreneur* (Crossing Press, 2001). And, according to this lifestyle entrepreneur, "Somebody who buys a franchise isn't a lifestyle entrepreneur."

Still, there's a lot of room in the definition of a lifestyle entrepreneur, and franchises and the closely related business opportunities are such an important type of small business that it's hard to ignore them. There are, depending on who is doing the counting and what definition they're using, somewhere between 1,500 and 5,000 different franchise systems in operation in the world at any given time. The

International Franchise Association, a Washington, D.C.–based trade group, estimates there are more than 320,000 franchised retail outlets in the United States accounting for $1 trillion in annual retail sales.[1]

Franchising as we know it is a combination of starting a new business and buying an existing one. This type of franchising is called business format franchising, a concept that dates back to the 1920s. Franchising is carefully regulated by state and federal laws. These laws define a franchise as a commercial relationship involving a licensed trademark, a required marketing plan, and payment of a franchise fee in exchange for the right to participate in the program. In this sense, many of the business opportunities, such as home-based party plan direct-sales programs, are not technically franchises. Most of these don't charge royalties, for instance. However, they are still regulated.

From a business standpoint, the key feature of franchising is the sale and use of a special system of doing business, as opposed to the older product franchising, which refers to the granting of rights to market a product in a particular territory. Use of a specific format or template is why McDonald's restaurants have a similar look and feel and menu the world over.

Franchising is generally less costly than buying an existing business and less risky than starting one from nothing. But it is more costly in both up-front and ongoing costs than starting a business. How much will a franchise cost you? With thousands of available franchises, the costs vary widely. The total investment required may range from a few hundred dollars, in the case of some direct-sales home-based business opportunities, to millions of dollars for some of the better-known food and service franchises.

A percentage of that up-front money is paid as a fee—$5,000 to $25,000 is typical for business-format franchises—to the company selling the franchise for the right to use its name and system. In addition, for most franchises you'll pay a continuing royalty of between 3 and 8 percent of total sales to the franchiser.

What you'll get in return likewise varies, but normally includes training in a tested business system, advice on handling business problems, participation in a joint marketing effort, access to cooperative purchasing, and other benefits. Some studies say franchises tend to generate more profit for their owners than nonfranchises—although no studies I know of have calculated their effect on the owners' lifestyles. And not all franchises are winners. Some place such heavy loads in the form of burdensome franchise fees and royalties and requirements to participate in costly cooperative buying schemes that they wind up benefiting primarily the franchiser.

You'll also lose a measure of freedom, as your franchiser dictates matters such as your facilities, signage, uniforms, advertisements, and many other aspects of your business. Perhaps Jane is right. But franchising can, clearly, satisfy certain lifestyle requirements. There is more freedom in owning a franchise than in being an employee, for instance. If you decide to look into franchising, there are numerous caveats.

Franchising How-To

What do you do if you're interested in a franchise? First, obtain the official document describing the terms of the franchise agreement. This is a legal paper required by federal and state franchise laws. It's known as the Uniform Franchise Offering Circular and describes the franchiser and the franchise program.

Legally, you have to receive a circular before investing in a franchise. In any event, you would be taking an unnecessary risk if you failed to read and understand—and have an attorney read and understand—the circular before investing. It will tell you, among other things, how long the company has been around, whether it's gone bankrupt or been sued, how much you'll have to invest in total, whether you'll have to buy supplies or products from the franchiser or some other designated supplier, and how much training you'll get. Many franchises used to be sold with protected territories, a fact that was spelled out in the circular, but this is becoming less common as we become saturated with franchises. You should also get names and contact information for other franchisees and find out from them what the company is like to work with.

Why so careful? Because, according to the Federal Trade Commission (FTC), every year tens of thousands of Americans lose their life savings to fraudulent franchise and business opportunities. In one case cited by the FTC, over a one-week period, 154 newspapers ran an ad saying: "Huge Profitmaker: $3,000 to $4,000 weekly income possible. All cash vending business. Prime groups available. Buy now and save. Zero down and qualified. Call Ed or Cindy or Lou at 1-800-192-1202."

Behind the ad was an outfit the FTC dubbed "the Wolf Group." From a Florida base, it sold vending and game machine businesses for $10,000 on up. The problem was that the profitable locations the company promised were, in many cases, promised to more than one entrepreneur. Others simply didn't exist. The company provided references who had been paid to lie. The would-be entrepreneurs lost millions.[2]

This is not to say there are not many legitimate franchise and business opportunities offered. Blue-chip franchises like McDonalds have made millionaires out of many people. It's questionable whether most McDonald's franchisees are primarily motivated by lifestyle considerations, however. A typical new McDonald's restaurant costs from $444,800 to $742,150, according to the company, not counting the $45,000 franchise fee. You have to have a minimum of $100,000 cash to get your foot in the door. And that means you have to personally have $100,000—McDonald's won't sell a franchise to someone who got the start-up cash from his rich uncle, best friend, or anybody other than himself.[3]

Business Opportunity Basics

Business opportunities like Amway, Herbalife, Pampered Chef, Creative Memories, and Discovery Toys are more to the point. These have provided part-time income, and in some cases more, for millions of people. The freedom of being a home-based, self-employed salesperson with flexible hours makes these and similar programs attractive to many lifestyle entrepreneurs. The multilevel or network nature of most of them allows you to make money off anybody you sign up for the program—and anybody signed up by the people you sign up—so your potential earning power can be significant.

This facet of the business opportunity industry has been around since at least the 1930s, when a Massachusetts company called Stanley Home Products began having individual salespeople hold in-home party demonstrations to sell its household cleaners, brushes, and mops. In 1951 an inventor named Earl Tupper hired an ex-Stanley saleswoman named Brownie Wise, who helped him set up the first of the soon-to-be-famous Tupperware parties.

The caveats applied to franchising apply equally to business opportunities. Before you send a check to sign up for any business opportunity, read their documents, talk to their other distributors, and have a professional such as an accountant or lawyer check it out.

There is one thing to watch out for, especially when it comes to business opportunity systems: commissions for recruiting. Most states make it illegal for a plan to pay existing distributors for recruiting new members. That is known as pyramiding and is prohibited because such plans have a tendency to collapse when no new distributors can be recruited, leaving the first people to join the pyramid rich (but possibly in trouble with the law) and the rest broke.

Here are the danger signs for multilevel marketing business opportunities:

- An offer to pay commissions for recruiting new distributors.
- A requirement that you purchase a lot of expensive inventory.
- Plans that promise you will make money through continued growth of downline—the term used for commissions on sales made by new distributors you have recruited—rather than through your own sales.
- Promises of enormous earnings using specific, spectacular figures—"$5,000 a week potential!"
- Claims of miraculous products.
- References who seem to speak too highly of their ability to earn money through the opportunity. They could be paid shills.

- High-pressure sales tactics. In particular, be wary of anyone who tries to get you to send money without seeing the circular describing the plan or without taking time to consult with advisors and think it over.

Does it sound as though most business opportunities are scams? You can't go that far, although it's certain that some are. Particular varieties, such as medical billing services and envelope-stuffing operations, are said by regulators to be especially popular among con artists. However, if you are cautious and determined, you can find a decent opportunity.

Jennifer Aston started answering internet ads and requesting information on various business opportunities after leaving her job as a training officer and deciding she would rather work from home with her family than return to the constant travel grind. "I was looking for something that didn't require me to go out and do home shows or classes," says the Florence, Alabama, lifestyle entrepreneur. "I didn't want to have to collect money, deliver product, or stock inventory. I wanted my start-up costs to be minimal because I didn't want the stress of having to pay back a loan. So that narrowed down my options tremendously."

Direct sales looked like the general direction, but Jennifer nixed cosmetics, nutritional products, spices, and other popular sales products. "A lot of direct sales opportunities require you to do home parties, shows, and classes. Plus some have quite hefty monthly minimums," she says. "I wanted something different. So it took me two years to find what I was looking for."

What she finally wound up with was a business selling theme party supplies and accessories and gift items. She's only been in business a short time, and the monetary rewards so far are falling short of her corporate paycheck. But thanks to her rigorous research, she is confident she will make financial sense of Onestopparties.com. "And, for my family, the lifestyle we live now is well worth the cut," she says. "This has been the most wonderful thing I've ever done."

Freelancing

In medieval times, I would never have been a freelancer. Back then, the term described a mercenary soldier available for hire to anybody who would pay his fee. Not my thing. More recently, freelance was a label applied to someone who sold services to an employer without any sort of long-term commitment. It was usually used in connection with freelance writers and artists. Nowadays, freelance work may mean anything from trimming trees to developing web sites. Whatever it means, it's common. A 1995 Bureau of Labor Statistics survey of U.S. workers labeled 8.3 million of them independent contractors—a close equivalent.[4] A few more findings from the BLS survey:

- These were likely to be middle-aged and older men who were "very satisfied with their work arrangements," according to the author of the BLS report. Does that sound like lifestyle entrepreneurs to you?
- They tended to be writers, computer consultants, insurance and real estate agents, and home remodelers—a diverse group of businesses.
- About half of the self-employed people were identified as belonging to this group, as opposed to being shop owners, restaurateurs, etc.
- They were more likely to work part-time, which BLS defined as fewer than thirty-five hours a week, than workers in traditional jobs. BLS interpreted this as a result of the older age profile of freelancers, and the fact that many were women who worked part-time while maintaining home and family responsibilities.
- It runs in families. Twenty percent of husbands and 32 percent of wives had spouses who were also freelancers.
- Three out of four worked alone, with no employees, although nearly one in eight had three or more employees.
- When asked why they were freelancers, only 10 percent of them cited an economic reason. Eighty-three percent said it was be-

cause they preferred it, enjoyed the freedom, and relished the flexibility.

- A whopping 96 percent expected their arrangements to continue indefinitely. That sounds like a perception of security, if not actual security.

Leave it to the government to cover you up with numbers, right? Still, I find many of the figures that came out of this study to be both illuminating of new truths and confirming of old ones. I've been in my job for fifteen years. How many other people do you know who have that kind of tenure? Yet I'm not unusual. Average tenure among freelancers studied by the BLS was 6.9 years, two years longer than the traditional workers they talked to.

How to Do It

That's a lot of information about the characteristics of freelancers, but not much on how to do it. The precise approach will vary by industry. Software developers tend to sign on for projects that may last months, while writers accept assignments that may take only a few hours. If you're interested in freelancing, here are some general things to consider:

- Plan to use the skills you employed in your previous profession or jobs.
- Make sure you have developed all the contacts you can before leaving your job to freelance.
- Don't burn your bridges. Often your first client is your former employer.
- Keep your costs low. Being home-based is the rule for freelancers—and why not? It's inexpensive and close to the refrigerator.
- Plan to make special efforts to get out of the house for social and professional interactions. Home-based freelancing can be uncom-

fortably isolating. Join clubs, take classes, and call people for lunch dates if your work doesn't require many meetings.

- Test your self-discipline before committing to the freelance life. Maximum freedom equals maximum responsibility. If you sit around all day watching soap operas and tape-delayed games played the night before, you'll be back in the job market in no time.

Freelancing, perhaps more than any other lifestyle entrepreneurship choice, is likely to be growth-constrained. Three-quarters of freelancers have no employees, making it hard for them to grow much. That creates a problem because, when you have no help, you must do everything. So freelancing requires exceptionally broad skills in micro-business management. Everything from ordering office supplies to strategic planning is up to you.

Moonlighting Made Easy

By daylight, Todd Kunkel works as a salesman for an aquarium supplies company in Ambler, Pennsylvania. By moonlight, he works in a building next to his house near Allentown, packing up exotic aquatic life for shipment to customers all over the nation who have ordered over his web site. From 10 A.M. to 4 P.M. Saturdays and Sundays, Todd stands behind the counter in Something Fishy, his weekends-only aquarium store.

It's a long workweek, totaling as many as thirty hours in addition to time spent at his regular job. But he's been at it for four years and shows no interest in giving up his moonlighting or in expanding it into a full-time business. Why? Part of the reason is that he's not certain he could make a go of it as a full-time lifestyle entrepreneur. Even his small operation requires $20,000 worth of exceptionally fragile inventory, and he's in competition in a national market against much larger dealers. "It's not a millionaire-making business," he says. "It's a tough industry."

Another reason is that, should he expand to a mall location requiring his full involvement and far larger investment of money and time, he fears he'll get burned-out on the business. Right now he likes working with fancy tropical fish, ordering them from places like Fiji, Tonga, Bali, and Java, and picking them up at the Philadelphia airport in person. He likes talking with the customers who visit his shop and pick his brains about reef aquariums, hermit crabs, and $40 coral fish. "I'm doing this," Todd says simply, "because I like to do it."[5]

Todd has a lot of company out there in the moonlight. A U.S. Department of Labor study of multiple jobholders in 1996 found that nearly 2 million people worked full-time at regular jobs and also part-time in self-employment. That's equal to about 1.5 percent of the total workforce, but one in four multiple jobholders.[6] Few were fish salesmen, however. Public administration and professional specialty workers such as teachers and professors were the most likely to hold multiple jobs. Nurses, firefighters, and police were also up there. Nor did they tend to work quite as hard as Todd. Thirteen hours a week was average on their secondary jobs, and their total workweek was a bearable forty-eight hours.

Todd's experience does, however, highlight several points about lifestyle moonlighting that should not be overlooked. They are:

- You will have to work longer hours—in effect, holding one and a quarter or more jobs—to keep moonlighting while working.
- You will retain the sense of security and regular paycheck that comes from having a conventional job.
- It's advisable if you can relate the work you do in your regular job to what you do as a lifestyle entrepreneur, as Todd did in his two aquarium-related ventures.
- You also want to make sure your lifestyle venture doesn't directly compete with your employer. Todd sells fish; his employer sells aquarium supplies excluding fish.
- You can take your lifestyle enterprise less seriously, and perhaps enjoy it more, when it's not your sole source of income.

Another thing you want to consider is the possibility that your employer will resent the division of your attention between wage work and moonlighting. You may have to work even harder at your job in order to avoid any hint of less-than-adequate commitment. When I was working as a staff journalist while freelancing on the side, I calculated the number of stories I ought to write for my paper every week in order to justify the salary I was being paid. I didn't tell my editor or publisher about this private arrangement I had with myself. I just did it. If I had an opportunity to freelance an article to a publication that might be considered a competitor, I told them about it. They never seemed to mind my moonlighting. Maybe that's because my personal production goal was enough to keep them happy. I know it worked for me.

SIX

Making Money

This book is not for the rich. I have avoided using as examples many people who could be described as independently wealthy. There are a couple of reasons for that. To begin with, there are a lot more people who aren't rich than people who are rich. And I hope that appealing to a larger market will help this book be successful.

On the other hand, why discriminate against the rich? If interviewing millionaires and billionaires such as Michael Dell, Jeff Bezos, and Ross Perot has taught me anything, it's that they have lifestyle issues too. So I haven't completely left out the moneyed among us. San Diego entrepreneur and inventor Harry Gruber made more than $100 million selling his internet start-up at the height of the dot-com investing frenzy. But his latest company, an on-line fund-raising service for non-profit organizations called Kintera, is clearly more related to his personal interests—now that he's rich enough and generous enough to legitimately be labeled as a philanthropist—than to any desire for a second huge financial score. Winemaker Charles Thomas is a retired obstetrician and gynecologist who did well enough to loan more than $2 million from his own pocket to Chateau Thomas Winery. Yet there is little doubt that winemaking in general, and Chateau Thomas in particular, is a lifestyle-oriented enterprise.

In general, what the lifestyle entrepreneurs I profile have in common, in addition to a desire to own a business subservient to their personal needs, is that they need to earn a living. Sometimes, they need it so much it's scary. "Fear and uncertainty are definite factors that come into play," says Karen L. Reddick, whose Denver home-based start-up provides administrative services to larger business. "What if it doesn't work out? What if I leave a stable income and then crash and burn trying to fly solo? Will my husband really support my decision in the long run, in the bad times?" she wonders. "It can be very terrifying, yet my heart knows which way it needs to go, and therefore my struggle continues."

Even lifestyle entrepreneurs who have a little more cushion have typically stretched close to their financial limits to get up and running. Holly Bolinger used personal ties from a banking career to help her borrow money to set up her Canton, Ohio, embroidery business. But she and her husband had to dip into their retirement funds to pay living expenses while the business got going. The business's failure to generate significant profit so far has been a burden. "This move has been hard financially in that we are so used to buying whatever toys we want," says Holly. "We are on a much tighter budget than before."

Holly, like many lifestyle entrepreneurs, became a business owner when she transformed what had been a hobby into a business. It needs to be clear, however, that lifestyle entrepreneurs are not just hobbyists. A business is a commercial establishment, enterprise, trade, or profession that is operated to provide a product or service and generate a profit. If you're living off your investments, you're not a lifestyle entrepreneur. If your activity only consumes money and isn't forecast to return any over and above its costs, it's a hobby.

Something called the profit motive distinguishes businesses from other activities. The profit motive could be described very simply as the desire to have some money left after you've paid for all the expenses of running your business. Of course, the Internal Revenue Service sees this as a more complex issue. The IRS uses a number of criteria to decide whether what you're doing has a profit motive. One of them is not, interestingly enough, the presence of profits. As long as you are regularly conducting transactions, producing income, and actively making good faith efforts to make a profit, Uncle Sam will usually rule that you are engaging in a business as opposed to a hobby. It matters because if you're running a business, you can deduct expenses such as the purchase of a computer or the costs of operating an automobile from your income, saving you money at tax time. Hobbies don't qualify for tax deductions.

Generally, according to the IRS definition, a hobby is an activity that is carried on for personal pleasure or recreation. It is not an activity entered into with the intention of making a profit. In determining whether you are carrying on an activity for profit, all the facts are taken into account. No one factor alone is decisive. Here is the list of things the tax authorities consider, quoted directly from an IRS publication:

- "You carry on the activity in a businesslike manner,
- The time and effort you put into the activity indicate you intend to make it profitable,
- You depend on income from the activity for your livelihood,
- Your losses are due to circumstances beyond your control (or are normal in the start-up phase of your type of business),
- You change your methods of operation in an attempt to improve profitability,
- You, or your advisors, have the knowledge needed to carry on the activity as a successful business,
- You were successful in making a profit in similar activities in the past,
- The activity makes a profit in some years, and the amount of profit it makes, and
- You can expect to make a future profit from the appreciation of the assets used in the activity."[1]

These criteria are slippery. What exactly is a "businesslike manner"? And there's no set number of them that are required for your activity to be classified as a business. But you'll have to satisfy many or most if you wish your activity to be considered as a business for federal income tax purposes. That can be a good thing. Doing so will allow you, for example, to use losses from your business (whether actual or paper, as in the case of depreciation) to shelter other income from taxation. So even a money-losing business can be a benefit to your wallet, as well as your lifestyle.

Financial Information

There is more to a human being than pulse, respiration rate, and blood pressure. And there is more to a lifestyle enterprise than cash flow, profits, losses, and net worth. But like the vital signs that indicate health or its absence in a human, these financial measures mark a business's viability or lack of it.

Financial reporting does play a role even in a lifestyle enterprise. Fortunately, there are just three main financial statements you need to know how to use in order to run your business. They are:

1. Cash flow. This report tells you on a quarterly, monthly, or weekly basis what money you can expect to have coming in, and what money you can expect to have going out.
2. Profit and loss or net income. This report tells you how much money you have left over after paying all your expenses, including everything from what it cost you to buy or produce your product to taxes and interest on loans.
3. Balance sheet. The balance sheet tells you whether you and your business are getting richer or poorer overall.

Cash Flow

The cash flow statement is the one you use to run your business on from day to day. Cash has been called the lifeblood of any business, and it's true that if you run out of cash you're very likely to be out of business soon.

Here's a statement of projected cash flow, by quarter, for the first year of a business that is expected to generate total sales of $100,000 its first year.

PROJECTED CASH FLOW

	Jan-Mar	Apr-Jun	Jul-Sep	Oct-Dec
Cash receipts				
Sales	15,000	20,000	25,000	40,000
Loan proceeds	10,000	0	0	0
Total cash receipts	25,000	20,000	25,000	40,000
Cash outlays				
Cost of goods	7,500	10,000	12,500	20,000
Selling, General and Administrative	3,750	5,000	6,250	10,000
Loan payments	0	0	0	5,500
Taxes	750	1,000	1,250	2,000
Equipment	10,000	0	0	0
Total cash outlays	22,000	16,000	20,000	37,500
Net cash flow	3,000	4,000	5,000	2,500
Opening cash balance	0	3,000	7,000	12,000
Cash receipts	25,000	20,000	25,000	40,000
Cash outlays	22,000	16,000	20,000	37,500
Ending cash balance	3,000	7,000	12,000	14,500

Note that the Sales portion of Cash Receipts ramp up steadily each quarter, topping out at $40,000—40 percent of the year's total—in the last quarter. This is typical of many businesses such as retail stores that are heavily dependent on holiday shopping. It's also not unusual for a start-up that expects to see its market and sales grow rapidly as it gets more established.

Another key item is the entry for Loan Proceeds. Without this $10,000, the enterprise would never get off the ground.

The first item under Cash Outlays, Cost of Goods (often abbreviated COGS), represents direct costs for procuring or manufacturing your products or, as the case may be, services. It will include buying raw materials to be converted into finished products, as well as direct labor costs such as wages for your production employees, if you have any. If your business is importing Mexican ceramics, for instance, COGS would include the cost of buying and shipping the imported pottery. If you were putting on cake-decorating seminars, your COGS would include the cost of renting the rooms, purchasing cake-decorating supplies, and baking the cakes.

Selling, General and Administrative (or SG&A), is a category for costs not directly related to producing your goods or services. That includes salespeople's salaries and commissions, sales trip travel expenses, advertising costs, and payroll for nonproduction employees. I've presented it here as a straight 25 percent of sales. That's a reasonable figure for some industries, but too high or too low for others. It's not necessarily accurate to figure it as a percentage that varies with sales. Some of these costs are likely to be fairly rigid, whether you have higher sales or not. You need to keep an eye on these expenses, since they can quickly become bloated.

If you jump down to the Loan Payments line under Cash Outlays, you'll see that you have a payment on the loan due in the fourth quarter. Assuming a second $5,500 payment is due in the fourth quarter of the second year, you will pay back a total of $11,000, including $1,000 or 10 percent simple interest, to whomever you borrowed this start-up capital from.

The Taxes line represents your withholdings for sales taxes only. Most states and local taxing entities have some sort of sales tax that sellers of products and services are required to collect and pay to the taxing authority. I'm putting this amount at 5 percent. You will also have to pay federal income taxes on your profits, of course. This venture is going to generate $29,000 in cash flow in its first year. Even after subtracting depreciation and other deductions, income tax may still amount to a few thousand dollars and you'll need to plan to have cash to pay it.

The Equipment line represents outlays for computers, fixtures, or machines you need to get up and running. For instance, if you plan to open a mobile dog-grooming operation, this amount might be required to purchase a second-hand van or to outfit your own vehicle for dog-grooming.

The next line, Net Cash Flow, is an important one. This cash flow statement shows positive cash flow every month. That's good, because when you spend more cash than you take in for very long, you are likely to be out of business. First-month cash flow would be negative without the $10,000 loan, it's important to note. The purpose of a cash flow statement is largely to spot periods when your cash flow is negative and take steps to reduce or eliminate them by cutting costs, increasing sales, obtaining a loan, or some other means.

The next three lines—Opening Cash Balance, Cash Receipts, and Cash Outlays—all come from other places on this cash flow statement. Opening Cash Balance is the amount of cash you are projected to have on hand at the beginning of the period. When you started out, before you got the loan, you had zero cash. At the beginning of each of the following periods, you have on hand the Ending Cash Balance from the prior period. The Cash Outlays and Cash Receipts entries are all carried down from the totals of the respective sections above.

The last line, Ending Cash Balance, is the one you want to watch like a cat watches a rat. Or, since problems in this line can be fatal to your business, perhaps the better analogy would be to watch it like a rat watches a cat. What you want to avoid is a negative cash balance at the end of any period. A negative cash balance means you are out of money. You can't pay any bills, purchase any materials, settle any debts, or make payroll. This statement shows a positive cash balance at the end of all the periods, which is good. To make sure that happens, many cash flow planners include another category, called Contingencies. If you try to think of everything, and add 15 percent more for Contingencies, you will have a good chance of accurately forecasting your future cash needs.

The last thing you should know about cash flow statements is that they should probably be prepared more frequently than quarterly. I've done it this way to be able to show a year's cash flow statement without including a daunting amount of detail. You should probably figure cash flow for each month the first year. Some experts say even each week. Either way, the principle is the same.

Income Statement

The income statement is the one most people think of when they think of business reports. After all, most people think businesses are all about profit. However, we've already seen they are also about cash, and we'll see in a few pages that they're about building monetary worth too. The premise of this book is that they can also be about improving lifestyle. There's more to business than you might think.

The profit and loss, or net income, statement is intended to tell you how much money you have left over after paying all expenses. It should include what it cost you to buy or make your product, including wages, materials, supplies, rent, and utilities, as well as items such as depreciation, taxes, and interest on loans. There are usually a lot more items on the cost side, but the income side may include sales and interest income. Here's a sample, simple income statement.

Sales is the top line of your income statement. This is a very important number. Sales are not the same as money in the bank, because you have to pay all your expenses out of them. But lack of sales is the most common reason for small businesses to fail. If you can keep the top line of your income projection high by generating adequate sales, you have a much better chance of making the rest of the numbers add up.

Note that the Sales figure comes from the cash flow statement. The $100,000 figure is the total of all the quarterly sales proceeds you are projecting for the entire year. Your statements—cash flow, income, and balance sheet—are all tied together in this way. Ideally, you will use

Income Projection

	Year 1	Year 2
Sales	100,000	125,000
Cost of goods sold	50,000	62,500
Gross profit	50,000	62,500
Expenses	35,000	25,000
Earnings before interest and taxes	15,000	37,500
Interest expense	500	500
Net income before taxes	14,500	37,000
Taxes	4,350	14,800
Net income	10,150	22,200

an electronic spreadsheet program to make sure that when you change a number in one of them—say, estimating that first-quarter sales will be $10,000 instead of $15,000—the result of the change shows up immediately in the income statement and balance sheet. This is not difficult to do with spreadsheet software. With a simple enterprise, it's not difficult to do by hand either.

Cost of Goods Sold is the same as the Cost of Goods Sold figure from your cash flow sheet. And again it's a cost that is subtracted from your sales.

When you subtract Cost of Goods Sold from Sales, you get Gross Profit. Gross Profit does not include the effects of other expenses such as selling, general and administrative costs, and interest outlays.

The entry on the next line, Expenses, includes the SG&A amount from your cash flow forecast, as well as some other costs. The chief one in this case is depreciation. Depreciation is a cost that is intended to reflect the loss of value that many items have over time. For instance, that $10,000 worth of equipment you purchased when you started your business will become less valuable as you use it and inflict wear and tear on it and as it becomes obsolete. Depreciation is useful for tax purposes because it allows you to reduce the amount of taxable net income that you show. That reduces your taxes. Yet you don't have to cut a check to anyone for depreciation. It's just for accounting purposes.

Most depreciation has to follow a schedule that allows you to deduct only a certain portion of the purchase price as a charge against your earnings each year. You might have to depreciate an asset for five or seven or more years, taking a percentage of the purchase price off your earnings every year until you have used up all of it. In this case, we're taking the entire $10,000 off your first-year income statement. That type of accelerated depreciation is something small businesses are allowed to do with some assets. The SG&A plus depreciation equals $35,000.

Earnings Before Interest and Taxes is also sometimes called your operating earnings. It includes all costs but financing costs, interest, and taxes.

Recall that $500 interest you have to pay on your loan? It goes on the next line, Interest Expense. You subtract it from the Earnings Before Interest and Taxes figure to get the next item, Net Income Before Taxes.

Net Income Before Taxes is the number you will use to figure your taxes. It's really important to some businesses, such as publicly held companies, that the pretax net income figure be as large as possible. Managers of these companies may do things, such as timing large purchases and payments, to make net income rise from quarter to quarter and year to year. Entrepreneurs, who don't have to answer to stockholders, may do just the opposite.

On to Taxes. For simplicity's sake, I have estimated taxes as 30 percent of your first year's Net Income Before Taxes and 40 percent of your second year's income. The 30 percent number is an approximate combination of the 15 percent federal income tax rate on $14,500, plus another 15 percent for combined Medicare and Social Security taxes. The number is higher the next year because the higher earnings will move you into a higher tax bracket. This approximation may be considerably wide of the mark if you have other earnings that place you in a different tax bracket. I'm assuming your lifestyle venture is a sole proprietorship, in which profits are normally taxed as ordinary income to the owner.

Net Income, the number at the bottom of your income statement, is the famed "bottom line." This is actually a paper or imaginary figure since some of the costs, such as depreciation, don't involve you cutting a check to anyone. You can operate a business for an extended period and earn a decent living without generating a penny of net income.

That is precisely the experience Hugh Daniels, the owner of Old Miner's Inn in Park City, Utah. "We've had positive cash flow for years, but I don't think we've shown a profit in all eighteen years," says Hugh. How has he survived? For one thing, the business provides many of the necessities of life to him. He lives in the inn, and his utilities, food, and many other costs are provided by the business. Depreciation has been another key part of the equation. Each year, he subtracts a portion of the value of the lodge and other assets from taxable earnings. As a result, he pays fewer or even no taxes despite generating spendable money from the business. "We're usually plus $15,000 or $18,000 a year, with probably $35,000 in depreciation," Hugh explains.

Balance Sheet

The cash flow statement tells you how much money you'll have on hand at any given time. The income statement shows whether you're operating at a profit or a loss. The third major financial statement, the balance sheet, tells you whether you and your business are getting richer or poorer. It does this by taking into account both your assets—the things you own—and your liabilities—the things you owe. Then it generates a figure for your net worth, or assets minus liabilities. If your net worth is negative, your business has consumed wealth instead of creating it for you. If the net worth is positive, you are creating wealth in addition to living a desirable lifestyle.

You'll need to prepare a balance sheet if you ever apply for a loan, take on a partner, or acquire an investor. Balance sheets are also useful to find out whether your business is building wealth over the long haul.

BALANCE SHEET

	Year 1	Year 2
ASSETS		
Cash	$14,500	$18,125
Accounts receivable	15,000	18,750
Inventory	15,000	18,750
Total current assets	44,500	55,625
Fixed assets	10,000	8,000
Total assets	54,500	63,625
LIABILITIES		
Accounts payable	12,000	15,000
Taxes payable	2,000	3,700
Total current liabilities	14,000	18,700
Long-term debt	11,000	5,500
Total Liabilities	25,000	24,200
Net worth	29,500	39,425
Total liabilities & net worth	$54,500	$63,625

This is a projected balance sheet, meaning it is an attempt to show where you'll be at some time in the future. In this case, it looks at the end of the year for the next two years. You'll notice that a lot of these numbers come from the other two financial statements. For instance, the amount of Cash you expect to have on hand at the end of Year 1, $14,500, come from the Ending Cash Balance shown for the final quarter of that year on your cash flow statement.

The Accounts Receivable figure is an estimate. Receivables are moneys owed to you by customers who have already taken delivery of the goods but haven't paid you yet. Based on your projected sales of $40,000 for the final quarter, it seems likely that you'd still have $15,000 of that left to collect from your customers. If you're doing a purely cash business, such as selling crafts at a flea market or running a restaurant, you won't have much in the way of receivables.

Inventory generally is possessed only by businesses that sell products. If you provide marketing services or book cruises, you won't have inventory. For retail stores, manufacturers, and distributors, inventory is a major issue. They want to have enough of it on hand to fill all orders quickly, but not so much that they can't sell it all quickly and at full price. It usually costs money to have inventory, since you may have purchased it with borrowed money or acquired it on credit from your suppliers. The longer it takes to sell the inventory, the more interest you will owe on the loans. On the plus side, inventory counts as an asset. Here I'm figuring inventory at about 15 percent of sales—an arbitrary figure, but one that is realistic for many businesses.

The Total Current Assets figure simply adds up your cash, receivables, and inventory. It represents the total amount of assets that are likely to be in spendable form within the near future—say, the next thirty to ninety days. Fixed Assets is another type of asset that isn't so easily converted into cash. It may represent a building you own, vehicles, machinery, or, in the case of this balance sheet, the $10,000 worth of equipment you purchased when you started the business. Note that this amount is smaller for the second year covered by this projected balance sheet. That reflects the effect of depreciation on your equipment. Just about all fixed assets experience depreciation—on paper at least. In fact, many of them, such as real estate, may increase in value over time. But the actual current value of assets isn't always shown on a balance sheet.

Liabilities relate to assets as the left hand relates to the right. In fact, the relationship is even tighter, since your liabilities must always exactly equal your assets in the world of balance sheets. Liabilities include bills that you are going to have to pay soon, such as rent, utilities, and payments to suppliers. These are represented by Accounts Payable. Taxes Payable is another bill you'll have to pay. The $2,000 I have entered for this year represents the current quarter's estimated federal income tax liability.

Total Current Liabilities is a useful figure for something called the current ratio. This is a simple, easy-to-calculate exercise that tells you a lot about your enterprise's financial health. You take the Total Current Assets figure and divide it by Total Current Liabilities. What's the right answer? Well, if your current ratio is below 1.00, you may be in serious trouble. It appears that the amount of cash you can raise on short notice is likely to be exceeded by the amount of bills you are going to have to pay soon. You may need to have a markdown sale to generate cash. In this case, dividing Total Current Liabilities of $14,000 into Total Current Assets of $44,500 gives us a figure of 3.17. In some industries that would be very good and in others only average, but it does suggest that this business is likely to be able to pay its bills for the near future.

Long-term Debt for this business consists of the $10,000 loan used to get started, plus the interest you'll have to pay on the loan. Notice that the $11,000 you owe this year shrinks to $5,500 the next year, since you have to pay $5,5000 on the loan.

Subtracting Total Liabilities from Total Assets gives you the figure of $29,500 on this balance sheet. That interesting number represents your Net Worth or Owner's Equity. It's the amount of personal wealth—over and above what you have earned and taken out as wages—that you have created by starting and running this business. The way to increase owner's equity is to decrease liabilities and/or increase assets. The owner's equity is a fluid number that depends entirely on assets and liabilities. It changes as necessary to make sure that the bottom line of the assets side of the ledger exactly equals liabilities.

Finding a Market

The only valid definition of "business purpose" is to create a customer, according to Peter Drucker, who is probably history's most
admired writer on managing an enterprise. Lifestyle entrepreneurs
might take issue with Drucker and add that the creation of a lifestyle
is also a valid purpose for a business. But you can't really argue with
the idea that a business has to have customers. Customers, after all, are
where sales come from, and without sales—that line at the top of the
income statement—none of the other measures of business health are
going to amount to anything. A strong sales figure, on the other hand,
can cover a multitude of weaknesses elsewhere in your business.
Either way, customers are the key. You have to have customers if your
lifestyle venture is going to survive as a business and allow you to live
the life you want.

Finding customers is another way of saying "finding a market."
That's a term you'll often run across when talking or reading about
starting and running a business. There are any number of ways to go
about finding a market and several considerations you'll have to take
into account when you're looking for one.

Perhaps the greatest entrepreneur of the internet is Jeff Bezos.
The founder of Amazon.com, he practically created the on-line
retailing business model. He survived the mass shakeouts of countless imitators and rivals and built a business that was generating bil-
lions of dollars in sales in just a few years and made him a
billionaire. How did he come up with the idea for Amazon? It
wasn't because he deeply desired to sell books. Instead, Bezos
noticed in the early 1990s that internet usage was growing at an
extremely fast rate. He deduced that these internet users represented customers that could be tapped through the medium. He settled on books because, with more than 1 million books in print, he
felt that selling on-line made a lot of sense. "When you have those
kinds of numbers, computers are incredibly efficient," Bezos told me
when I interviewed him in 1997. "You can build something that
can't exist anywhere else."

The point of the Bezos story is that he started by looking for customers. Then he came up with a business that could sell them something effectively. That doesn't mean lifestyle entrepreneurs should do the same thing. It does mean that customers are so important that if you can find them, you can build a successful business around them.

For a lot of lifestyle entrepreneurs, personal needs rather than surveys of growing internet usage tend to drive the decisions of what they are going to sell and to whom. By personal needs I mean the individual lifestyle entrepreneur's desire for something that isn't sold, or isn't sold well. Many businesses have been built around the idea of providing some product or service that the entrepreneur wanted and guessed that others would also.

The big question for a lifestyle entrepreneur who wants to build a business around a personally felt need, of course, is whether enough people feel strongly enough about this need to be able to support a profit-making enterprise. In business terms, this refers to the scalability of the enterprise. You may be able to find one or two people who want what you have to sell, and you may be able to provide it to them profitably and while maintaining or enhancing your lifestyle. But can you find a larger market? And can you serve it efficiently and profitably?

The ability to forecast sales is all-important when it comes to starting and running a business. It's also just about impossible to do with much accuracy. That goes for sophisticated multinational organizations as well as for solo operators of lifestyle ventures. You just don't know what's going to happen, and so you always wind up guessing. Guess wrong, and you could be out of business.

One of the most tempting things for a new business owner to do is to commit what is called the 1 Percent Fallacy. This happens when a business owner looks at the size of a market and says, "If I can just capture 1 percent of that, I'll be sitting pretty." One percent doesn't sound like much, granted. But that doesn't mean it's easily obtainable. If you could high jump 1 percent of the distance from here to the moon, you would be the greatest high jumper in history. You would also be in orbit in outer space.

So how do you figure out what your sales are likely to be? Research. If you think that a lot of florists would be interested in hiring you for your special skills at designing bouquets for multiethnic holidays and events, you can call a few flower shops and ask them. A big business that is preparing to spend, say, $100 million to develop a product that it plans to roll out globally may invest millions in surveys, focus groups, and ethnographic studies to reduce the risks that its planned product will fall flat. You don't need to do that, even if you could, but you should do what you can to gain information that will help you forecast sales. If all the flower shops you call say they'd be interested, you can probably be sure there is enough demand to justify printing up some business cards and spending a few weekends trying out your planned venture. If everybody says no, even after you've called every flower shop in town, it's time to reassess your commitment to this idea and, perhaps, move on to another.

One thing nobody can do is predict the future with regard to a specific product or business. Coca-Cola spent more than $4 million interviewing almost 200,000 consumers to test a new formulation of its flagship soft drink.[2] Yet the rollout of New Coke in 1985 is still one of the most disastrous new product introductions in history. Some people say Coke just asked the wrong questions; others say the New Coke debacle simply illustrates the failings of modern market research.

Still, when it comes to business results, you can often make better predictions than Coke did. For instance, many direct mail marketers use a standard of 2 percent when estimating what the response will be to a mailing. However, this can vary from much smaller to much larger. An unlucky and unskillful direct marketer might get no responses even to a sizable mailing, while a well-done direct mail piece targeted to a group of people who are predisposed to buy—perhaps because they are existing customers—might get a return rate of more than 40 percent.

My own experience is that about 15 percent of my proposals for articles are accepted overall. About half of my proposals are mailed, usually electronically, to existing customers. About 25 percent of those get accepted. The other proposals go to editors I haven't worked with before, and only 2 or 3 percent of those are accepted. Your mileage, of course, is going to vary. The only way to be sure is to try.

Predicting Profits

Profit is what's left after you've paid everybody. The math is straightforward: Profit equals income minus outgo. It's usually pretty simple for a lifestyle entrepreneur to calculate whether a sale or a day or a month or a quarter has been profitable, simply by counting up income and taking away costs. But what you really need to be able to do is to determine in advance how much profit you are likely to get from a sale, a customer, or an entire business. That job is a little more complicated, involving the forecasting of income and outlays, but it's very important to at least attempt it.

The most straightforward way to predict in advance whether a business or an individual transaction will produce a profit is to add up all the costs you expect to incur and find out what price you would have to charge in order to have some money left when it's all over with. This is known as the cost-plus method. It's popular, but harder than it seems, because you can't reliably predict in advance either the expenses you will encounter or the revenues you will generate. For instance, while the sales price is marked on this book, it is likely to be sold through a variety of different channels including retail bookstores and direct mail and bulk sales to organizations, each of which will be charged a different price. There is no way for me or my publisher to know precisely in advance what the mix of these shipments will be. So we can't both precisely and accurately predict what the revenue figure will be, even if we knew how many copies would be sold.

The same thing happens with expenses. Until you have some experience with producing and marketing your product or service, the only thing you can reliably predict about what it will cost you is that your best estimate will not be quite on the money. When you are forecasting the costs for starting a new business, there are always many unforeseen expenses. You may find that you need an expensive license in order to start or that the piece of equipment you planned to lease is now available only for sale, requiring a much larger up-front outlay of cash. As Gilda Radner's Roseanne Rosanna-Danna character used to say on *Saturday Night Live*, "It's always something."

Here are some of the common expenses many lifestyle ventures will have to accommodate:

- advertising
- automobile expenses
- bank charges
- cleaning
- debt repayment
- education and training
- entertainment
- equipment lease payments
- insurance
- interest charges
- internet service
- legal and professional fees
- maintenance costs
- mortgage payments
- professional dues
- rent
- salaries
- sales commissions
- supplies
- taxes
- telephone service
- travel
- utilities

Your profit-predicting plan doesn't have to take all of these into account, but you should look at this list to make sure you aren't leaving something out. I have learned through long experience at making financial plans that there is no way to think of every cost or expense. Therefore, every cost projection must include an amount for unforeseen contingencies. This amount will vary from 10 percent to 30 percent. If you add a contingency cost item equal to 15 or 20 percent of the total outlays, you will probably be in good shape to handle the inevitable surprises.

It's very difficult to guess in advance what your costs are going to be when you are just starting up. Even after you've been in business for a while, it still isn't easy. Every year is a new one, and you face new challenges that are hard to budget for because they are new. One thing you can do to get a good idea of what costs should be is to check the experiences of companies like yours. A service called BizStats.com provides a great deal of free, very useful information in this area. A quick look at one of BizStats's charts of expense ratios for small corporations will show you that the typical architectural firm spends 3.3 percent of its revenue on rent, 0.6 percent on interest charges, and 20.9 percent on salaries and wages. There are dozens of similar charts for many different fields. You can access BizStats at www.bizstats.com.

If you look at nothing else from BizStats, take a look at the net income averages. They show that small corporations in the accounting field typically report net profit margins of 13.6 percent, meaning they keep as profit 13.6 cents out of every dollar they bring in. Building materials retailers, on the other hand, hang onto just 4.3 cents out of every dollar, while building contractors have profit margins of about 5.7 percent. These profit averages are good guides when it comes to evaluating whether you'll be able to meet your financial needs with a lifestyle venture.

Profit Problems

One of the most common and enduring fallacies about earning a profit is that increasing the dollar volume of sales or units sold will help. That's often true, but just as often not. There are two things this idea is based on. The first is that, if you are making a dollar by selling one of an item, you will make two dollars by selling two of that item. So far, so good. But that principle doesn't always hold. There may be only one customer who is willing to pay enough for your item to maintain that dollar profit. Or it may be that other customers are more expensive to sell to—for instance, they may live farther away, so shipping costs eat up your dollar. Often, more sales mean more profits. But don't assume that they do.

The second foundation for the higher-volume fallacy is the idea that as you produce and sell more, your costs will go down and your profit margins will go up. This was spectacularly true in the case of Ford Motor Co. After Henry Ford threw the switch to activate the 120,000-employee River Rouge plant, he was able to produce far more cars than before. This meant, among other things, he could cut better deals with materials suppliers and more efficiently utilize the investment in expensive tool and manufacturing equipment. Increased efficiency cut his costs and enabled him to cut prices on the Model T. That made the car affordable to many more people, which increased Ford's sales and profits, allowing him to cut the price further, making the car affordable to more people. This type of virtuous circle is the ideal of the business plan based on exercising efficiencies of scale.

Not all businesses benefit from economies of scale, however. Let's say you have always loved to cook, and you realize your dream of working as a chef when you open a high-end restaurant in a small city. Business is good enough that your dining room is full most nights. Your profit per dinner is only moderate, however—a problem you trace to the fact that you pay too much for your ingredients, which is your biggest cost after labor. You reason that with a larger kitchen and dining room you could buy more food, get bigger discounts, and earn more profits. If you increased the number of diners you hosted, you could cut prices. In pursuit of economies of scale, you take out a large loan to open a bigger restaurant. You get lower average food costs, but the new, larger dining room isn't nearly full enough. So you cut prices. Unfortunately, a low-cost restaurant is already well-established in town, and you can't pull in enough diners to cover the costs of servicing the loan. As a result, you run out of money and are forced into bankruptcy.

This unfortunate scenario is too common among business owners who feel that what works for another business will work for them. Take care before you try to grow in search of economies of scale or any other phenomena that appear to be helping out another company. Every company is unique in many ways, and each has its own optimum route. Lifestyle entrepreneurs can lose a lot of lifestyle trying to manage a rapidly growing business. It pays from a lifestyle standpoint to look carefully and skeptically at any plan for making more money by increasing sales.

Understanding Your Business Model

The key to making the right decisions about the proper scale for your business, the price you should charge, and the profits you should expect is understanding your business model. A business model is an explanation of how your enterprise is going to generate profitable revenues. At bottom, all business models describe the furnishing of a product or service in exchange for pay. Some are simple: A computer consultant's business model might explain that he charges small businesses an hourly rate for setting up their computer networks. Others are more complex: A radio station broadcasts its content for free, making money by selling airtime to advertisers. In this case, the service it is providing is exposure to its listeners. It's the same thing, just hidden behind a couple of layers.

One of the critical factors in any business model is the break-even point. This is the point at which the gross profit you are generating from sales is enough to cover your fixed expenses. The interesting thing about the break-even point is that, beyond this point, sales begin to produce profits. On the other hand, if your sales fall below this level, your lifestyle venture is losing money.

Break-even analysis starts with two bits of information: your fixed costs and your gross profit margin. Fixed costs are expenses you have unrelated to sales. They include rent, interest, insurance, office supplies, maintenance, and any other outlays you have to make whether you sell anything or not. Your gross profit margin is the difference between your sales and the cost of those sales, expressed as a percentage of sales. If you buy T-shirts for $6 and sell them for $9, your gross profit is $3. Gross profit margin is 50 percent. Once you've got these two numbers, divide costs by profit margin. For example, if fixed costs for your beachside T-shirt shop run $4,000 a month and your gross profit margin is 50 percent, your break-even point is $8,000 in sales. You can use break-even analysis to decide whether to carry a particular product, invest in an ad campaign, hire more people, and make many other business decisions.

Pricing Your Product

Hardly any decision is more vital than the price you decide to charge for your product or service. For any business, the price charged affects the size and other characteristics of the potential market. It also profoundly affects how much profit the venture will generate, both per individual sale and in the aggregate. The powerful effect of setting prices is not to be underestimated. Consider, if you are charging $10 for Sunday brunch at your country cafe, and your costs per brunch customer equal $7.50 a plate, then you are generating $2.50 profit per brunch customer served, or a 25 percent gross profit margin. You raise the price to $12.50, a 25 percent increase. Your profits double to $5 a plate, while your profit margin increases to 40 percent.

The flip side of higher prices is that, as you raise prices, you generally reduce the number of customers who are able or willing to pay the increased cost. The question is, How much of a deterrent will the higher price be? It turns out that a higher price has to be quite a deterrent in order to reduce your total profits. Here's how it would work for our country cafe owner. Let's say that, at $10 a plate, the cafe sells an average of 16 brunches every Sunday. At $12.50 a plate, the crowd falls to just a dozen brunchers. But because of the powerful leveraging effect of higher prices, the inn actually makes more money serving 25 percent fewer brunches. Here's how it looks in a table.

Brunch Price	Number of Diners	Revenues	Costs	Profits
$10.00	16	$160	$120	$40
$12.50	12	$150	$90	$60

Let's take a look at the other approach: Cutting prices. Cutting prices often looks tempting. The theory is that you will attract more customers and the higher volume will more than make up for the lower price. But competing on price is a dangerous game, especially for small enterprises. Let's say our cafe owner decides to cut the price on the brunch by a dollar, just 10 percent. At $9, the brunch pulls in 25 percent more customers. Because the per-plate price is lower, revenues climb just 12.5 percent, to $180. Meanwhile, costs per plate stay the same, so they increase 25 percent along with the number of customers. The result is that you'll wind up making less money, while working harder serving four extra brunches. Take a look at the following table.

Brunch Price	Number of Diners	Revenues	Costs	Profits
$10.00	16	$160	$120	$40
$9.00	20	$180	$150	$30

At what point, you may wonder, do more customers add up to more profits for our discount brunch-seller? The answer may be surprising. After cutting prices just 10 percent, the number of diners who have to be served to increase profits increased by nearly 69 percent. At $9 a brunch, you'd have to serve 27 brunches—11 more—to beat the $40 profit you did at $10 a plate. Your extra earnings? A measly 50 cents. Here's the table in case you find this hard to believe:

Brunch Price	Number of Diners	Revenues	Costs	Profits
$10.00	16	$160	$120	$40
$9.00	27	$243	$202.50	$40.50

To return to our earlier table showing the effects of higher prices, you'd have to drive off half your clientele before you had any effect on profits. Here's the revised table showing how you can make just as much money, doing half as much work, by raising prices 25 percent:

In the real world, it's not this simple. You may be able to get a break on your food costs by ordering more, for instance. And you have to take into account fixed costs, such as rent or mortgage payments, plus

Brunch Price	Number of Diners	Revenues	Costs	Profits
$10.00	16	$160	$120	$40
$12.50	8	$100	$60	$40

the wages you have to pay your kitchen help, if you have any. These have to be accounted for no matter how many brunches you serve.

There is also a limit on how far you can raise prices. Sometimes you can't raise them at all without driving off so many customers that you're worse off than before. But as a general rule, you should be slow to cut prices with the goal of increasing profits. It is worth looking into opportunities to pass cost reductions on to your customers, since this won't reduce your profits and may increase your market. But cutting prices without matching cost reductions is a game in which the arithmetic tends to work against you.

The sensitivity of a group of customers to changes in price is called price elasticity. Price elasticity varies depending on your product, your service, and your competitors, among other things. For luxury goods—such as Sunday brunches—higher prices may cause demand to fall off sharply. Bigger price tags for essentials, such as medical care, tend to affect demand less. But as a general rule, there is often less elasticity than you might think.

When Patti Glick first began her home-based business as The Foot Nurse, she didn't know how to price her services. A friend who had experience booking brown-bag seminars for corporations suggested $150 per seminar, so she tried that price to start with. "That rapidly changed," Patty says. "I realized I was not the typical 'Come in for an hour, do my thing and leave.' I did foot measurement afterward, so I was really there for two hours."

So she raised her rates. "People still booked me," Patty reports. After five years, she now charges $300 an hour—twice what she started at. And since she's charging for two hours, the effective rate per seminar is four times the initial level. At forty or fifty seminars a year, Patti is making a nice income for only a few hours' work a week—each seminar takes her about four hours including travel time. Now she'd like to start another sideline, providing private foot-care counseling in her home, and she has to consider price all over again. Her gut feeling is to charge $30 per half-hour consultation. Even without travel time, that's an effective rate less than half what she's getting for the seminars, but she feels confident she will know when and how to raise prices later on if it seems feasible. "I've had people say that's too low," Patti says, "but it feels good for now as a way to start."

One rule that I have used for pricing my services is to try to set your prices so that about 15 percent, or one in six, of the potential customers or opportunities you encounter decide not to use you because your price is too high. This is a tip I got from somewhere else, and I don't know exactly how the 15 percent rule was arrived at. However, it is a good one. If about one in six of the people who contact you with an interest in buying from you think you are charging too much, then you are meeting the price expectations of the overwhelming majority of your possible customers, while not charging so little that many people would pay more.

Picking Winners, Losing Losers

One of the most powerful concepts in business is that not every customer is worth selling to. This potent truth is expressed in many different ways, such as "You can't be all things to all people" and "Feed the rich and grow poor; feed the poor and grow rich." The basic idea is that, especially if you're a small business owner, you have to pick the people you're going to sell to and not try to serve the rest.

One of the most well-known statements of this rule came from a late nineteenth-century Italian economist named Vilfredo Pareto. Pareto noted that 80 percent of the wealth in Italy was owned by 20 percent of the people. Since then, Pareto's Principle has been applied to everything from time management to quality control. The 80–20 Rule, as it's also called, has proven to be both highly flexible and pretty reliable. For instance, you very likely will find that 80 percent of your sales come from 20 percent of your customers. Also, 20 percent of your customers are likely to create 80 percent of your service calls, complaints, and returns.

Once you identify the one-fifth of your customers who are generating most of your sales, you can often greatly increase sales and profits by focusing marketing efforts on them. Or, when you have tabbed the 20 percent who are causing most of your problems, you can stop calling on them and save yourself a lot of headaches.

The Pareto Principle does have some limitations. For instance, it's not unheard-of to find that the 20 percent of your customers who are generating 80 percent of your sales are also generating close to 100 percent of your profits. A tougher Pareto problem is posed by the question, What should I do after I've gotten rid of the 20 percent of my customers who are generating the most problems? Should I then identify the 20 percent of my remaining customers who are generating the most problems? How long should I continue this? Clearly, you will eventually arrive at the point of diminishing returns when applying the Pareto Principle to choosing the people you will do business with. If nothing else, continually paring away the customers (and suppliers, vendors, employers, or whomever) you work with will eventually leave you with a single customer. That's something you probably don't want.

Despite its limitations, most lifestyle entrepreneurs will find a great deal of inspiration in the Pareto Principle. It will allow them to improve their sales and profits, reduce their costs, and increase the performance of their business in many ways. Not the least of this is that the Pareto Principle gives a solid foundation for efforts to stop working with people and organizations that are having a negative effect on your business or your life.

SEVEN

Funding a Lifestyle Venture

When you are considering starting a business for lifestyle or any other reasons, you will very soon run into a roadblock. That roadblock is made of money or, more accurately, the lack of it. In short, you will either learn on your own or be told by someone else that it takes more money than you have to start a business, and so you are not going to be able to get yours started. You will discover that for you to open the antiques boutique you want to run, you must have hundreds of thousands of dollars for inventory, fixtures, and working capital. Or you will be told by someone with a lot of experience in the field you want to get into that, in order to do it right, you will need a million dollars, or more, just to get going.

While it is important to be realistic when starting a business, it is also important not to be too pessimistic. Many, if not most, successful lifestyle entrepreneurs proceeded with their plans in spite of others' warnings. They refused to be deterred by the fact that their planned venture appeared to lack adequate financial resources. To a considerable extent, entrepreneurship involves a leap of faith. There is no amount of research, calculation, or advance planning that will remove all risk from a business venture. The same is true of financing. No matter how much money you have to start your business, you cannot escape the possibility of failure.

A well-known recent case of a well-funded failure is Webvan. This on-line grocery store raised more than $800 million in funding but lasted only a few years before seeking bankruptcy protection in June 2001.

But one of the most enduring examples is Trilogy Systems. This company was started by entrepreneurial legend Gene Amdahl. He was the lead designer of the System 360 mainframe computers whose success is responsible for much of IBM Corp.'s prosperity. After leaving IBM, Amdahl created the industry of IBM-compatible computers by starting Amdahl Corp. in 1970 to make and sell inexpensive computers that worked with IBM printers, software, and other gear. Amdahl Corp. was a huge success and by 1980, when Bill Gates was an unknown and Michael Dell was in high school, Gene Amdahl was the archetype of the high-tech entrepreneur. That's when he raised $230 million to start another company called Trilogy Systems that was supposed to produce advanced semiconductors. To make a long story short, Trilogy was a bust. Despite Amdahl's experience, reputation, and ability and nearly a quarter-billion dollars—a huge amount then and now—it failed.

Now let's take a test. Which of the following successful enterprises started with less than $10,000 in capital?

1. Apple Computer
2. Dell Computer
3. Domino's Pizza
4. DVDEmpire.com
5. Lillian Vernon
6. Mary Kay Cosmetics
7. Microsoft
8. Nike
9. The Limited
10. Yahoo!

The answer is: All of them. Steve Jobs and Steve Wozniak sold a Volkswagen van and a calculator to raise $1,350 and start Apple. Michael Dell began Dell Computer in his college dorm room, buying components to assemble into computers only after he'd received an order for one. Domino's founder Tom Monaghan and his brother bought their first pizzeria in 1960 for a reported $900. Lillian Vernon used a wedding gift of $2,000 to start her mail-order house. Mary Kay had a recipe for skin cream and $5,000 when she started her beauty empire. Bill Gates and Paul Allen started Microsoft in 1975 as an informal partnership. Nike founder Philip Knight swooshed into business selling shoes from his car with $1,000 behind him. Les Wexner borrowed $5,000 from an aunt to open the first Limited store. David Filo and Jerry Yang were Stanford engineering students when they began indexing web pages as an unpaid hobby that would become Yahoo!, the top site on the internet.

I am remarking on these examples because, of course, they are remarkable. Unfortunately, you can't count on starting a global empire with a few thousand dollars. But you can count on having a chance to start a viable lifestyle enterprise with that much, or even less. There are countless examples of other, smaller businesses that were begun with similar or smaller sums. I included DVDEmpire.com on this list specifically to make that point. Jeff Rix started the on-line seller of DVD movies in 1997 with a combination of $6,000 in funds from his partner, his father, and his own savings. You may have never heard of DVDEmpire, since they are just one of many smallish sellers of digital movies over the web. But at this writing, Jeff, who is only twenty-eight, oversees forty-eight employees and sales in excess of $20 million a year. And there are many, many other entrepreneurs who met their financial and lifestyle needs with varying degrees of success, after starting out with similarly modest financial backing.

Looking for Financing

In many cases, the search for funding for a lifestyle venture is a short one: You look in your own pocket and if the money is there, you're in good shape and your search is over; if it's not, then you are in bad shape and your search is also over. That may not be happy news, but it's often true. The reason is that, when it comes to financing as in many other matters, lifestyle businesses are different. In Chapter 1, the term "lifestyle entrepreneur" was specifically defined as referring to businesses that were not primarily intended to ever be sold for a capital gain, a characteristic that made them relatively unattractive to many of the usual sources for business financing.

Of course, some lifestyle ventures do create significant wealth and are able to attract outside capital. Joyce Meskis, owner of the Tattered Cover Book Store in Denver, employs more than 300 people at two bookshops, a pair of coffee shops, and a restaurant. Joyce studied mathematics and English in college, planning for a career as a university professor. Before starting her teaching career, she realized that what she really wanted to do was sell books, something she'd been doing part-time while in college. "One morning I woke up and something said, 'You idiot, you've been doing what you love all these years. Why not get serious about it?'" Joyce recalls. That was a quarter-century ago, and today Joyce is one of the most influential independent bookstore owners in the country. She's also able to borrow money from the bank whenever she needs to.

But lifestyle entrepreneurs like Joyce are the exceptions. You are like her in that you have good personal reasons for starting your business. But other people don't normally risk financial resources to start businesses unless they can expect financial rewards in return. It's not pleasant to consider the likelihood that other people aren't as interested in funding your lifestyle as you are, but it's probably true.

That's the bad news. The good news is that you may well have more financial options than you are aware of. Your own pocket may well include a variety of viable sources of money, from personal and retirement savings to second mortgages and even credit cards. If you include the pockets of your family and friends, you may find you are able to raise enough money to set yourself up more than adequately. And, while Wall Street may not come pounding on your door to buy stock or lend you money, outside financing sources such as trade credit and traditional bank loans have helped many lifestyle entrepreneurs get under way.

There are a surprising number of places people go to for money to start new businesses. Banks are just one, and while they are the most popular place to borrow money, they are by no means the best for many businesses. Take at look at these potential sources of financing for lifestyle ventures and see if one or more looks like a possible solution for you.

Your Personal Savings

This is just what it sounds like: the money you have in your checking and savings accounts, mutual funds, retirement accounts, and so on. It may also include proceeds from a second mortgage or home equity loan, a lump-sum severance payment from an employer, proceeds from an insurance settlement, or an inheritance.

One good thing about using personal savings is that you may not have to ask anybody for permission to use the money. I say "may" because although the money may be your personal savings, other people such as your spouse and children may have a strong interest in what happens to it. You should consult with them before investing your life savings or taking out a second mortgage to back a lifestyle venture.

Personal savings got Jane Pollak started as an egg decorator nearly thirty years ago. "I did a crafts show which cost me maybe $25 at the time, so there wasn't any need to finance that," Jane recalls of her first business effort. "And I didn't have the typical start-up costs of renting an office and getting equipment. I already had a telephone, and there were no computers then, as far as I knew. It was all stuff I already had."

Eventually, Jane did spend more serious money on her enterprise, performing a major renovation on her home to create an office and studio. By then, several years into her life as a business owner, she was able to fund the renovation out of savings. Jane was helped by the fact that egg-decorating is an inexpensive art form. "It's eggshells and dyes," she notes. "I could make hundreds of pieces for under $100."

Family and Friends

Loans and investments from people you know or are related to is the second-biggest source of start-up funds for companies. Family-and-friends loans may come with low or no interest rates, or may even take the form of outright gifts. Terms may be equally generous, and may even be "pay me back when you can."

In 1977 it was tough for any woman entrepreneur to get a bank loan, much less one who had sunk all her savings into a bookstore that she had just closed, recalls Joyce Meskis. So Joyce turned to family and friends for loans to purchase the Tattered Cover from its previous owner. Later on, she was able to qualify for bank loans, and today the company is as bankable as any. Many lifestyle entrepreneurs can tell similar stories.

The downside of family and friends financing is that, if the business doesn't work out and you can't pay back creditors and investors, you may damage your relationships with people who are close to you. So avoid accepting money from family and friends without specifying in writing when and how it is going to be paid back. If you can't come up with a firm arrangement that seems workable, it's probably best to pass on this idea.

That was what Pasadena, California, fashion entrepreneur Stephanie Turk did when a friend offered to help finance WearUnder, her start-up that designs and manufactures lingerie for large-busted women. The amount in question is "a nice sum," according to Stephanie. "But we don't see eye-to-eye on a lot of things." Although she could really use the money, she doesn't plan to take on this particular investor. "It's one thing to be friends," she explains, "and another to be business partners."

Customers

Your customers can do a lot to bankroll your business. One way is by asking customers to make up-front payments before receiving their product or service. Marketing and public relations counselors, management consultants, professionals such as attorneys, and others commonly request half of their fee in advance, for instance. If you can make a few advance sales and collect enough deposits and prepayments, you may be able to bootstrap your business entirely without outside financing.

Donna LaVoie had some savings when she started her home-based strategic communications company in August 2001, but she waited until she had signed her first client—on terms calling for advance payment of a third of the project fee—before announcing the start-up and hiring her first employee. "You don't need a bunch of money," the Swampscott, Massachusetts, entrepreneur says of her financing strategy. "You just need a client."

Suppliers

Any time a supplier sells you something and delivers it without collecting full payment, that supplier is effectively financing your purchase. Purchasing supplies, materials, or inventory on thirty-, sixty-, or ninety-day terms is the same as taking out a loan for that amount. The fact that the supplier doesn't charge you interest, require you to fill out a lengthy loan application, or do much more than demand a clean credit history makes supplier credit the most readily available and widely used form of financing for all businesses.

Bank Loans

Lifestyle ventures can get bank loans, although not all do, and many of those that do aren't thrilled with the process or the results. Stephanie Turk collected an impressive-sounding $80,000 bank loan in the form of a line of credit guaranteed by the Small Business Administration, a federal government agency that, among other things, helps small companies get bank loans. But she spent almost a year pursuing that loan before actually receiving the funds in August 2000. Furthermore, she had applied for a $200,000 loan and had done her budgets for WearUnder using $150,000 as the expected proceeds. The loan "was enough to get me going but not what I asked for," Stephanie says. "We're day to day and week to week now, but I think we'll get over the hump."

The Small Business Administration's many loan-guarantee programs are practically tailor-made for lifestyle entrepreneurs seeking as much as $1.5 million on terms of up to thirty years and interest rates as low as 4 percent. Later on, as The Tattered Cover's Joyce Meskis and many other entrepreneurs have found, a record of borrowing and repaying money can make it much simpler to do business with banks on conventional terms. However, the SBA application process is, as Stephanie found, notoriously lengthy and paper-intensive. And, while SBA guarantees can do a lot to encourage a banker to loan money to a company that would otherwise not be considered worth a loan, it's not foolproof.

Whether you are seeking a bank loan with SBA help or on your own, the key is to understand how bankers' minds work. They are not interested in making your life easier, saving the world, helping to provide a useful product or service, or even in making a financial killing. They just want to earn a market rate of interest on a loan and, above all, to be repaid. Bankers demand collateral, as a rule, but the flip side of that rule is that the last thing most of them want is your collateral. What they want you to show them is that you will have the cash flow to pay the principal and interest.

Being able to think like a banker helped Holly Bolinger of Canton, Ohio, when she was downsized from her job as a commercial lender, a career she had been in for twenty years. In addition to being a veteran banker, Holly was an enthusiastic and skillful seamstress. She and her husband had considered opening a business doing custom embroidery years earlier, just before their second child was born, but weren't ready to make the financial commitment. "It is something I enjoy and does not feel like work," Holly says, echoing the sentiments of lifestyle entrepreneurs everywhere. "So after being downsized, this was immediately the field I looked into again."

Holly had some savings, but with the computerized sewing equipment and software costing many thousands of dollars, acquiring the tools to get Logomotion Embroidery up and running would require a loan. "Years of negotiating commercial loans and an inside knowledge of financing really helped," Holly reports. "We used some retirement money that we had set aside as cash flow, but basically financed most of the equipment through the bank I had worked for. Because I was a known entity, we were able to get a great rate, easy terms, and a quick turnaround time."

Credit Cards

Examples of entrepreneurs who finance their start-ups with a fistful of credit cards are legion. Ex-model Maura Peters of Los Angeles created the first batches of her nonallergenic Essential Stuff beauty products with $5,000 in savings and the proverbial stack of plastic. It started off fine, when she sold all of her first test runs. "Then suddenly you're buying equipment. And you need space." Maura shakes her head. "We went into some serious debt. But now it is all coming back, and the potential is huge."

Of course, it doesn't always happen that way. Some people even say it's unethical to finance a start-up with credit cards because of the relatively high risk that a business will fail, leaving the card issuer with a bad debt. Certainly, it may not be the cheapest way to bootstrap a start-up. Making minimum payments on the credit cards used to pay monthly bills at Wendy White's Arizona Sled Dog Inn in Flagstaff stressed the company so badly that Wendy had to go back to work full-time as a lawyer, while still running the inn on the side.

But credit cards can work if you don't overdo it. Robin Knepp began All About Dogs, her pet training and day care company, with credit cards. Careful management allowed her to eventually qualify for an SBA loan.

Leasing Companies

You can lease almost anything you could buy, from a car to a pizza oven. Leasing is a convenient, simple, fast, and popular way to acquire the equipment you need to operate your business. You can't get working capital by leasing, but you can free up cash to use for working capital. The applications and financial requirements made by leasing companies are generally less onerous than bankers'. The downside is that when all the payments are added up, leasing usually costs more than outright purchase. But leasing can still be a cost-effective as well as convenient financing approach, especially when it comes to technology gear such as computers that become obsolete quickly. Kai Adams and his partners leased a $30,000 point-of-sale computer system, a $3,000 commercial dishwasher, and other costly restaurant apparatus when starting Sebago Brewing, a microbrewery in Portland, Maine. "They do all the legwork, they contact the vendor. We just make a monthly payment," Kai says. "And we don't have to lay out all this cash. It's pretty painless."

Asset-Based Lenders

Receivables are generated by any business that deals on anything but a cash basis with its customers. There are lenders known as factors, who will pay you cash now for the right to collect on your receivables when they become due. The service isn't free. Factoring will cost you a fee of 1 percent to 2 percent of the amount you would otherwise receive, plus you'll pay interest at the prime rate or above until the factor has actually received what is owed by your customers. The advantage to you as a cash-strapped business is that you can receive that money now, without the risk of bad debts or the wait to collect. This kind of asset-based borrowing is a standard practice in many industries. Refactors are similar companies that combine smaller quantities of receivables into the million-dollar quantities that factors look for. You can look into whether a factor or refactor could help your company by checking with a commercial bank or looking in the phone directory under "Factors."

Angel Investors

Angel investors are individuals who exhibit a combination of personal wealth and willingness to take risks that makes them endeared to entrepreneurs. Angels are generally perceived to be willing to take risks that other investors would shun. Sometimes they invest in ventures because they want to see them succeed, more than because they want to make a pile of money. They may back an entrepreneur because they like that person or because the entrepreneur reminds them of themselves at a younger age. They may offer more generous terms than other investors, especially when it comes to demanding management control.

By having more than purely financial considerations at heart, angels closely resemble lifestyle entrepreneurs themselves. However, I have run across relatively few lifestyle entrepreneurs who have tapped the angel investing world. Perhaps that is because of the difficulty all entrepreneurs experience in finding angels. As private individuals who aren't professional investors, they don't hang out shingles. They do attend venture capital conferences, network with university small business development centers (SBDC), and get many referrals from accountants, attorneys, and other professionals. Contacting your local SBDC, networking with professionals who may advise angels, and otherwise putting yourself in the way of an angel can work wonders.

When Rich Owen and Todd Wichmann were trying to start their business, they needed several million dollars to purchase the Oxydol brand name from its owners. "Rich and I didn't have any personal wealth accumulated to pull this off," says Todd, who was then twenty-nine, two years younger than his partner. "So we had to go out and find high net worth individuals—angels." The angel investors helped them purchase Oxydol, and they formed Redox Brands to try to pump some life back into the name. It worked better than anyone would have guessed. Oxydol's sales tripled and then tripled again in two years. Today the co-CEOs have twenty-six employees and have also purchased rights to Biz bleach. "We did this against everybody's advice," notes Rich. "But so far, it's made sense for us." Without angels, none it would have happened.

Partners

Many partnerships are formed of one person with technical expertise and one with prowess at marketing. But many others are composed of one person who has either or both of those competencies, and one whose primary contribution is financial or the equivalent. Famous motherly advice states that it is as easy to fall in love with a rich man as a poor one. Lifestyle entrepreneurs who are willing to take on the potential stresses of partnership might heed the same advice.

Stephanie Turk was looking for a garment factory to manufacture her lingerie when she contacted one that was about to close its doors for lack of business. Sensing an opportunity, she arranged to take the plant owner on as a partner. That way she got the manufacturing capacity she needed at a lower cost than she would have gotten at another plant, which amounted to an increase in her working capital.

Employees

The people who work for entrepreneurs are as interested as the owners when it comes to making sure the business endures. That's why employees can sometimes serve as sources of capital. You can sell partial ownership to employees in exchange for contributions from their paychecks. You can ask them to take lower wages to help the business prosper. You can bring them on as equal partners with a say in decisions. If you need money to start or expand a business, consider looking for it among your enterprise's employees.

Corporations

Big companies sometimes invest money in an enterprise that, for one reason or another, they want to see succeed. Jeff Colborn was working for a high-tech company when he quit to become an entrepreneur developing fuel cell technology as an alternative energy source. "The reason I chose this field was because I wanted to do something that not only was a commercial success but also had benefits for future generations," says Jeff, who holds a Ph.D. in nuclear fusion technology.

Jeff funded the first couple of years of Metallic Power's operations with the help of government research and development contracts. After a few years and a few prototypes, he was able to land $6.6 million in investments from investors including two of America's largest public utilities, Hydro-Quebec and Allete Inc., formerly known as Minnesota Power. Companies like Allete, which has 14,000 employees, may give money to entrepreneurs like Jeff for a variety of reasons. In this case, they wanted access to the cutting-edge fuel cell technology Jeff was developing. They might also be interested in obtaining a marketing channel, forestalling a competitor, or even supporting a worthy cause. Not all big companies are interested in funding smaller ones, but if you have the right kind of venture, it's worth looking into.

Venture Capitalists

Venture capitalists (VCs) are people and institutions that help finance young companies that are relatively high risk but also offer relatively high returns. A lot of lifestyle ventures are risky, but relatively few offer higher-than-average returns. How high? A typical VC would demand at least a 35 percent compounded annual rate of return on an investment in a new company. VCs also want to cash out pretty quickly, in two to five years, usually through the sale of the company to another, larger firm or through a public stock offering. Neither option is likely to appeal to lifestyle entrepreneurs, since they necessarily entail loss of control of the company. Speaking of control, venture capitalists like to exercise it. A VC will typically demand some combination of majority ownership of the company, one or more seats on the board of directors, and even a new CEO selected by the VC.

All these reasons are why lifestyle entrepreneurs and venture capitalists rarely wind up doing business together. Even Rich Owen and Todd Wichmann, whose effort to resuscitate old brands has more profit potential than most businesses, got a cold reception when they approached venture capitalists with a request to fund their purchase of Oxydol. "This was in spring of 2000," recalls Todd. "It was the heyday of the dot-com era, and we pitched this idea of launching the oldest name in the old economy. Everybody was too enamored of the dot-coms to talk to us."

Public Offerings

The Initial Public Offering (IPO) was an icon of the 1990s business owner. Twenty-something entrepreneurs were transformed into millionaires overnight when investors bid up prices for newly issued shares of their dot-com enterprises. At the time, we knew that this probably hadn't happened often, if ever. Now we know that it likely won't happen again soon, if ever. It's also clear that the steep costs and accounting, legal, and financial requirements for an IPO rule it out for the vast majority of lifestyle firms. For one thing, it's so expensive to complete the paperwork that you can't do a conventional IPO cost-effectively if you want to raise less than several million dollars. IPOs are not likely financing solutions for lifestyle entrepreneurs.

Financing

While I've been pretty negative about the prospects for conventional big-money financiers backing a lifestyle venture, I don't mean to say it can't happen. Harry Gruber, for instance, is a medical doctor and serial entrepreneur who starts companies because he loves doing it. One of the half-dozen or so enterprises he has begun was a company that transmitted audio and video over the internet, and it attracted investments from Microsoft, General Electric's NBC subsidiary, and AOL Time Warner. AT&T and MCI WorldCom joined it in collaborations. Then in 2000, the company was purchased by a large internet services company for $2.8 billion. That's billion with a *b*. Harry's share amounted to $146 million. Yet today Harry is happily engaged in yet another start-up. He definitely considers himself a lifestyle entrepreneur. "I still work 100-hour weeks," he says. "But it's not really work. I find something fun to do and then get someone to pay me to do it. My job is my passion."

In another example, David Wheeler started his company for the most nonfinancial of all reasons: His father had been mysteriously murdered, and David, a database expert, created a software program to help police detectives analyze the large volumes of poorly organized, loosely formatted tips and other information that typically accompany a crime investigation. In 1991, ten years after his father's death, David started InfoGlide Software Corp. in Austin, Texas, to refine and market the software. Eventually David's invention was used by many law enforcement agencies, including the FBI's antiterrorism arm, and InfoGlide became a thriving business, employing as many as seventy people. InfoGlide software was also adopted by insurance company antifraud investigators, and today is employed by on-line auctioneer eBay to detect crooked bidding practices. Along the way, it attracted a great deal of investment, including $13 million in venture capital financing in 2000. Ironically, David never applied his creation to his father's case, which was solved almost twenty years after it occurred when an organized crime hit man confessed to the slaying.[1]

A Basic Rule of Financing

Finance is a complicated and fast-changing arena where there are many rules, and those rules are constantly being rewritten. But there is one fundamental principle that hasn't changed much over the years: that is, the term of the loan should fit the purpose. This seems pretty simple, but it will help you to figure out the best way to finance your business as well as give you some insight into the thoughts of those who are providing you with financing. In practice, it means you should avoid taking out a long-term loan to pay for something you'll use for a relatively short term. This is why you take out a thirty-year mortgage to buy a house, which should last that long, but you only take out a loan of five years or so to buy a car.

For a lifestyle entrepreneur, this suggests that it's probably not a good idea to use a personal credit card—a short-term loan—to pay for equipment you'll use for a long time. The reason is that you could probably get the money to buy that equipment much less expensively by seeking longer-term financing, such as a bank loan or equipment lease.

Sweat Equity

One of the most important forms of financing for a lifestyle entrepreneur is known as "sweat equity." If you learn nothing else about financing, you should understand sweat equity. Properly speaking (if that can even be said of such an earthy term), sweat equity is the value you add to a business by working without pay or for less pay than your labor is worth on the open market.

Sweat equity can amount to a lot. If it would take $50,000 a year to hire someone to do what you do for $25,000, you are adding something like $25,000 in value to your company every year by not taking the full $50,000. Over time, that adds up remarkably quickly, especially if you carefully use sweat equity to expand or improve the efficiency and effectiveness of your business. Throw in the savings from not having to pay interest on money borrowed to make the improvements sweat equity funded and it's clear that sweat equity is one of the most powerful tools available for financially helping your business.

Of course, you have to have money to live on. Many lifestyle entrepreneurs who are funding their start-ups with sweat equity earn living expenses by continuing to work as employees, full-time or part-time, so they don't have to rely on earnings from their early-stage lifestyle venture to put food on the table. There is nothing wrong, by the way, with a business that doesn't turn a hefty profit from day one. Even Microsoft didn't earn a profit its first few years in existence.

Continuing to work while launching a lifestyle venture can be very effective. Canadian Paul Cartwright indulged his love of sports in 1997 by starting Sports Celebrity Marketing, a Georgetown, Ontario, company that matches retired and locally popular athletes with marketers who don't have millions to get Michael Jordan or Tiger Woods on board. Paul kept the company home-based and used his personal savings to get it going. But for the first three years, he kept his full-time job as a salesman.

Since then, Paul has been working full-time signing endorsement and appearance deals for the likes of Paul Henderson, a retired hockey player tremendously popular in Canada, and Manny Sanguillen, a

Major League Baseball catcher who retired in 1980 but is still beloved by Pittsburgh Pirates fans. Was working two jobs worth it? "This is a whole lot more fun," Paul says. "Sports is a passion. I grew up watching these guys. They were my childhood heroes. I can always go back and sell boxes of this and cases of that and do a good job. But how do you get passionate about coffee filters or ketchup?"

For a lot of lifestyle entrepreneurs, a lack of passion for what they are currently doing for a living is one big reason they are looking for a lifestyle venture. But when what you are currently doing can provide you with the financial means to pursue that lifestyle venture and, eventually, make it your only occupation, then earning living expenses from a job while building sweat equity in your own business becomes a much more attractive concept. It can be a very flexible and effective means of getting around the financial roadblock that looms so large in the beginning of most ventures, lifestyle or otherwise.

PART THREE

Making It Work

EIGHT

Picking Your People

One of the big reasons Stephanie Turk is a lingerie-designing lifestyle entrepreneur rather than an engineer for the State of California is that she wants to pick the people she works with. She had grown frustrated with the government bureaucracy and felt management didn't appreciate her ideas and contributions. Then she says, "I went in to work one day, and my supervisor said the wrong thing on the wrong day. I'd had enough, and I decided I'd rather do something else."

Stephanie is not the only lifestyle entrepreneur who was motivated by people to become a business owner. Many other lifestyle enterprise owners cite difficult bosses, imperious customers, and unlikable coworkers as critical forces pushing them into business ownership. Once they become business owners, lifestyle entrepreneurs find that they like being able to make decisions about who they will work with and how.

Jill Morgan, of Keller, Texas, started Purple House Press in 2001 because she couldn't find affordable copies of children's books she had loved as a girl. "It's been a great move," she says. "My birthday this year was one of my best, simply because I woke up and felt good about what I was doing," she said a year after starting her venture.

Jill revels in working with children's book authors such as Leonard Kessler, the writer and illustrator of *Mr. Pine's Purple House*, a 1965 title that was one of her childhood favorites. She gets a thrill out of helping parents who would like to have copies of books like *Mr. Pine* to read to their children, but can't afford the $300 price of a collectible first edition. Another big payoff is that Jill gets to pick who she works with when it comes to doing the actual publishing. After contracting out the prepress work to other firms for her first few titles, Jill decided not to use outside services and to start doing the work herself. "I didn't feel people were putting enough effort into making the books look good," she explains, "and that's my favorite part of the job."

When you run your own business, you make the decisions about the employees you hire, the suppliers you buy from, the customers you sell to, the bankers you bank with, your business neighbors, and almost any other person you are likely to run across in the course of a day. Of course, you don't have total freedom in any of these areas. Here are a few of the factors limiting your choices:

- Equal employment and anti-discrimination laws limit your freedom to hire and fire employees.
- There may be only a few vendors who, for geographic or cost or other reasons, are viable choices to supply your business.
- Your customers' ability and willingness to pay for what you have to sell limit your ability to choose customers.

But the fact that there are limits to your ability to choose the people you will work with isn't the point. The point is, you can have a lot of influence in all of them. If there's a customer you can't stand or a supplier who drives you wild, you don't have to put up with them because a supervisor a thousand miles away says you have to. If you can do without the customer, if you can find another supplier, you can find someone more to your liking. If you elect to choose the people you work with, you can.

You can see examples of this in large companies as well as small firms. For instance, for many years Toyota was considered almost exclusively a maker of economy cars. Its customers were after cheap, reliable transportation, and the company had grown to worldwide prominence for its ability to supply those features. Several factors, including American import quotas that limited the number of cars Japanese makers could bring into the country, motivated Toyota to find customers among buyers of high-end cars. In 1983, the company's chairman, Eiji Toyoda, ordered Toyota marketers to find a way to tap the luxury car market. Out of that decision the Lexus brand was born, and today Toyota, through Lexus, has grown into one of the world's leading suppliers of autos to luxury car buyers.

For a lifestyle example, look at Denver printer Brad Stillahn. Brad has begun developing international clients for his label-printing business specifically so he can take business trips from Denver to places such as Brussels, where he had gone to a trade show not long before we spoke. "I could have chosen a segment of business that was domestic and traveled back and forth to Chicago," he noted. "Instead, I'm heading to Alaska in a couple of weeks, then Australia."

For the same reason, Brad has targeted the coffee industry as a segment he wants to market to. Sure, it's a industry well-suited to his business of supplying specialty retailers with labels. But that's not his only concern. "Right now, it's traveling around the world," he says. "And there are coffee plantations all around the world."

Picking Employees

I confess that I am not one of those people who needs people, at least as far as my business life goes. I am perfectly happy laboring in solitude in front of a computer, day after day. I do enjoy interviewing people on the telephone or in person for articles and books, and I like occasional travel to meet with an editor, conduct an interview, or make a public appearance for a book. I am moderately active in my local freelancer's association. And I definitely enjoy spending many more hours a day with my wife and children than I probably would otherwise. But when it comes to picking the people I do business with, my biggest choice is to not have many people around most of the time.

Many lifestyle entrepreneurs feel likewise, or nearly so, especially the numerous home-based entrepreneurs chronicled in these pages.

However, Chicago career counselor Arlene Hirsch cautions would-be lifestyle entrepreneurs against assuming, without any evidence, that they're going to love working alone all day long. "Some people are extroverts. They need to have other people around," she warns. It's not uncommon in Arlene's experience for home-based entrepreneurs to find the experience too isolating. "They actually need the structure of having other people around," she says. "Those would be people who might buy a store or get a part of a shared office space."

Some lifestyle entrepreneurs take a middle path, working most of their time alone but employing one or two people, perhaps part-time. Home-based business golf consultant and speaker Cheryl Leonhardt says of her single employee, "That's it, and I like it that way."

Other lifestyle business owners work from home without employees, but don't exactly spend the day alone. Take, for instance, Lesley Spencer who left her job as public relations and tour coordinator for Dave Pelz Short Game Golf School after her baby was born. Now she works from her Austin, Texas, home running Home-Based Working Moms, a professional association and on-line community she founded in 1995, personally pursuing her organization's stated goal: "Bringing working moms closer to their children."

After leaving his life as an investment banker, Mark Abouzeid tried being Mr. Dad to his new offspring. "After six months, I quickly found out I'm not capable of doing that," Mark says. So instead he got into the internet, offering information consulting services to clients from his villa in Tuscany, Italy. He hires men to help him harvest the olives from the ancient trees on his property. His wife works on a different floor of the villa, managing the on-line travel site she set up. Mark spends most of his work hours in front of a trio of computers and is happier being a part-time Mr. Dad. "I take my daughters to the bus in the morning, talk to my neighbors over coffee, and work the olive trees in my spare time," he says. "I don't make appointments for quality time because it all is."

Personal preference isn't the only guide to choosing people to work with, especially when it comes to employees. Laws and regulations in most countries govern the employee-employer relationship. In the

United States, for instance, a number of laws prohibit employment discrimination based on race, color, sex, religion, national origin, age, or disability. They include:

- Civil Rights Act of 1964. This legislation prohibits discrimination on the basis of race, color, religion, sex, and national origin.
- Age Discrimination in Employment Act of 1967. This specifically outlaws age-based discrimination against people forty years old or older.
- Americans with Disabilities Act. This 1990 law prohibits discrimination against disabled workers if the workers are qualified to do the job.
- Equal Pay Act of 1963. This law makes it illegal to pay men and women unequal wages for equal jobs.

This is only a list of major federal legislation. Laws and regulations control discrimination against pregnant women, against people based on their sexual orientation, and others. Employers may face a "wrongful discharge" civil lawsuit from an employee who, although not covered by any of the anti-discrimination rules, feels he or she can make a case that the employer violated a fair labor law. Employers can get in trouble with federal, state, or local regulators if they violate laws setting rules for paying minimum wages or overtime pay.

The good news is, many of these laws will not apply to the typical lifestyle entrepreneur. The Equal Pay Act applies to most employers who have even one employee. But the employment discrimination provisions of the Civil Rights Act only affect employers with fifteen or more employees, the federal age discrimination act covers employers with twenty or more employees, and the Americans with Disabilities Act is relevant only to companies with fifteen or more employees.

U.S. entrepreneurs can learn more about employment discrimination laws and regulations by contacting the Equal Employment Opportunity Commission, www.eeoc.gov. Many states, provinces, and even cities have their own anti-discrimination laws as well. Check with your local department of labor or equivalent agency for details, and, if there is doubt, consult with an attorney who specializes in employment law.

Hiring for Lifestyle: Ways to Reduce the Paperwork

Having employees is a burden, no question about that. As an employer, you are responsible for making sure that someone gets a check on payday. If you have ever been told by a boss that the money you were expecting wasn't coming, you know that it is simply unacceptable to be unable to make payroll. That's a lot of pressure, and it is a form of pressure that many lifestyle entrepreneurs choose to do without.

The paperwork and other overhead of being an employer can also be challenging. Employees may have to have tax documents prepared, withholding withheld, insurance policies and pension plans administered. You may have to place and pay for help-wanted ads. Then you'll have to sort through applications, conduct interviews, and check references. Applicants who live in another town or state may request payment for travel expenses. You'll have to train employees so they can be productive, and you'll have to oversee them as they do their work. Since tax-related paperwork is one of the burdens you will certainly encounter if you have employees, let's take a look at some of the U.S. tax forms and filings that are required if you have even one employee:

- Form W-2. This is a form that reports the amount of wages you paid an individual employee during the prior year. It includes information about amounts you have withheld from the employee's paycheck for various taxes. You have to file one for each employee and provide copies to him or her.
- Form W-3. This is a form you use to transmit to the Internal Revenue Service information about wages you have paid and taxes you have withheld.
- Schedule H. This is a document that people who have household employees such as babysitters, housekeepers, yard workers, and drivers have to fill out to report the wages.

- Form 1099-Misc. This is a form you may have to fill out and file if you paid someone to work for you as a subcontractor rather than as an employee during the course of the year.

And there are more. For instance, many states and some cities require employers to fund unemployment insurance for workers. You'll have to pay these taxes and file forms, sometimes quarterly or even monthly, when you send in the payments.

By the time you get through with it, the overhead of having an employee makes it clear that, no matter how productive your employees are, it's not a 100 percent gain to have them helping you out. There are, however, ways to have employees without spending too much time on their affairs.

Employee leasing lets you take on workers without taking on all of the hassles. The employee leasing firm is the actual employer, responsible for handling payroll, taxes, insurance, and other matters. You pay the leasing company, which pays the employees. Leasing is a little more costly than do-it-yourself employing, but it's less trouble for you.

Temporary employees are useful if you only need extra help for a short while. Seasonal businesses, such as retailers who do most of their business around the holidays, rely heavily on temps. You get temporary employees from temp agencies. As with leasing, the temp agency is the official employer so you're relieved of doing anything more than cutting a check to cover wages, taxes, and administrative fees. Temps may be trained in useful skills, but they aren't always. The best thing about temps is that when the need has ended, you don't have to fire or lay off anyone, pay severance, arrange for outplacement, or do anything other than send them back to the temp agency to await their next assignment. Hiring a temp is, among other things, a good test to see if you are ready to have employees.

Part-time employees can give you the help you need without quite so much of the hassle or expense of full-time permanent employees. Since they're working fewer hours, your total commitment for wages is lower. Also, part-timers aren't as likely to demand costly benefits, such as medical insurance. You can find part-timers among the ranks of students, senior citizens, disabled citizens, moonlighters, and even other lifestyle entrepreneurs. Part-timers are helpful when you're trying to increase production, get some help with administrative matters, or extend the hours of a retail business's operation.

Each summer I hire a college intern to help me out with my work, which, in addition to benefiting me, provides a training opportunity for a deserving journalism student from the local university. I have them work fifteen or twenty hours a week, approximately half of which they spend working on their own at their own home or other location and half with me in my office. I pay them hourly about what they would earn at an entry-level journalism job, but don't offer any benefits. And I cap the internship length at eight weeks, so we can both have some time off during the summer. College interns are motivated, but often less trained than people who've been in the workforce for a while. Sometimes, however, you can find an older person who is going back to college and would like to work as an intern. You can find student interns by contacting your local college or high school.

"Outsourcing" is a buzzword among human resources professionals at big companies. These firms are finding it makes good sense to have certain specialized job functions handled by someone other than an in-house employee. So instead of employing a full-time bookkeeper, you might have someone come in for a few days to do the monthly payroll and inventory. This is tailor-made for lifestyle entrepreneurs, who may lack the expertise to handle their own accounting and computer systems maintenance, among other functions. You can find people to outsource work to in the Yellow Pages. Check references and make sure the service provider is willing and experienced at working with smaller, less formally organized companies.

Family members can be a labor pool for you too. You can put a spouse or child on the payroll and, without changing your overall family income, move to a lower tax bracket. You may also be able to provide benefits, such as fully deductible health insurance or a tax-sheltered pension plan, to a spouse when he or she is an employee. Paying your kids is a good way to help them without being subjected to federal estate or gift taxes. As a kicker, wages paid to an under-eighteen child by an unincorporated business aren't liable for Social Security taxes.

Keep careful records of the type and amount of work done by any family member for pay. Don't pay them more than you'd pay someone else. As a general rule, anytime you are uncertain about tax regulations, you should consult with an accountant or attorney who is competent in these areas. A final word about hiring family members: My wife and I used to share a home office that was so small (this was a New York City apartment) that if one of us wanted to open a file cabinet drawer, the other one had to leave the room. Yet, we are still married today. One thing that may have helped was that, while we worked together, we didn't work for the same company. She was a full-time employee who telecommuted from home a couple of days a week. I was engaged in my own, separate lifestyle business. That was helpful, I think. When you're working in the same company with a family member, it can be difficult to make joint decisions, establish lines of authority, and draw boundaries between work and personal life. Even harder than sharing a closet-sized office.

The Promise and Peril of Partners

If the people who earn a living investing in new businesses are right, you have a lot better chance of making it if you don't try to go it alone. Professional investors prefer to see teams of more people atop a young company, believing that two or more heads are better than one when it comes to solving the problems of a start-up. Entrepreneurs, however, don't usually do it that way.

By far the majority of companies are sole proprietorships, where one person owns the company and makes all the decisions. According to the U.S. Census Bureau, nearly 75 percent of all U.S. companies are sole proprietorships, around 20 percent are corporations, and the rest are partnerships. When it comes to companies that don't employ anyone other than the owner or owners, there are more partnerships than corporations. Yet sole proprietorships make up even more—over 90 percent—of these smaller enterprises.[1]

It's not hard to understand why lifestyle entrepreneurs would want to avoid partners. Having someone else on board can hinder free action, a prime motivator of many lifestyle entrepreneurs. Partners in a general partnership, the most popular form of partnership, can legally commit the enterprise to something such as a lease or purchase contract without the other's approval. Both are liable for debts the partnership may engender. And if one of them wants out, the other may have to come up with a cumbersome amount of money to buy him or her out—perhaps even being forced to sell the business to do so.

Yet there are good reasons why lifestyle business owners should consider taking on a partner. One is money. Many partnerships consist of one partner who primarily provides financial backing, while the other runs the business. Another reason is complementary skills. Perhaps the most typical partnership is one pairing an entrepreneur who possesses marketing skills with one who has technical know-how. One partner may have a long-range vision, while the other excels at day-to-day management. One may be good with people, the other with machines. Partnerships may also receive more favorable tax treatment. They allow you to spread the workload around, even take an occasional vacation. And you'll have another person who's just as vested as you are to bounce ideas off of.

To improve the chances of a partnership being a success, choose someone whose skills complement yours, whose goals are similar, and who is willing to share decision making. Colleagues, customers, suppliers, professional service providers, lenders, and even competitors may be good sources of partnership candidates. But usually, for lifestyle entrepreneurs in particular, a partner is a friend, relative, or other close associate whose ties precede the decision to go into business. Often, a partner's encouragement is the spur to a lifestyle entrepreneur's decision to start a business.

Your marriage partner or significant other, if you have one, is going to be your partner to some extent in any business you engage in. A lot of lifestyle ventures are actually organized as partnerships between spouses. Many started their companies specifically because of a desire to work alongside a spouse or partner. Is that a good idea? Kathy Marshack, author of *Entrepreneurial Couples*, notes, "Since six out of ten marriages in America end in divorce, it is probably wise for entrepreneurial couples to take this fact into consideration when developing their life and business plans." She quickly adds that this statistic doesn't mean you should plan for divorce, since that may be a self-fulfilling prophecy. But it's worth thinking about the effect that having a spouse for a partner may have on your business and your marriage.

Of course, it can work out beautifully. Minneapolis entrepreneurial duo Anne Warfield and Paul Cummings started their company, Impression Management Professionals, as a vehicle to jointly realize their ambitions. "About five years ago, my husband and I set down a life plan," says Anne. That plan called for them to work in the same business. They don't, however, do the same job. She is a speaker, trainer, and author, traveling to many places to give seminars on using conversation to create an impression. His primary job is marketing.

They are like many successful partners in that they have well-defined areas of responsibility. Other things you should do to increase the chances of a successful partnership include:

- Talk everything out first.
- Get it in writing.

There are lots of lesser things to consider when putting together a partnership, and formal documents describing the terms of a partnership can fill many legal-sized pages. But these are the basics. If you discuss in advance who will make which decisions, how income and ownership will be divided, and the best response to every possibility you can think of—from great success to utter failure and every side trip in between—you will reduce the chances of finding yourself in a situation where one of you adamantly wants one thing, while the other just as adamantly wants the opposite.

When you've decided how you'll set things up, it's important to put it down on paper. Misunderstandings and forgetfulness can occur even in the closest partnership. Committing the terms of the arrangement to written form clarifies things immensely. And, while the purpose of a partnership document isn't to trick anyone into signing away anything they don't want to, having a permanent record to refer to will at least remind the partners that they once agreed to a particular setup and help defuse feelings of being misled.

"Don't skip the couple talk," advises Anne Warfield. "The income may drastically change, and you have to be able to deal with that. You may have to decide whether to sell the house and invest the money in the business. You need to know how far are we in this together, and what are we both willing to do. Sometimes they just assume that the other is on the same plane, and you can't do that."

Picking Customers

Just saying no sounds pretty easy, but it's not always so when it comes to a lifestyle entrepreneur's customers. Even when you strongly suspect that a customer is not going to work out in the long run, the pressure to just say yes can be enormous. Take the case of Susan and Barry Brooks, respectively a former schoolteacher and homebuilder, who partnered with some friends to open a retail cookie bakery. After a few years, they started franchising the concept and grew to fifteen locations. But as they grew, their quality crumbled, the franchisees proved uncontrollable, and their partnership—and friendships—fell apart.

Sadder but theoretically wiser, they moved from Athens, Georgia, to Tempe, Arizona, and started another company, Cookies from Home, that would mainly do mail-order sales in addition to a single retail store. They'd learned their lesson about franchising, resolving not to do that again. However, they still proved better at getting growth than managing it. The first Christmas, orders came in at fifteen times the normal rate, far more than they could deal with. Yet they took every order. "We baked twenty-four hours a day," Susan recalled. That wasn't enough. Phones went unanswered, shipments went unshipped, orders went unfilled, and, in the pressure-cooker atmosphere, critical employees quit and major customers soon followed. Cookies from Home hung in there. The Brookses hired management consultants to advise them on what they needed to do. They installed upgraded phone and computer systems capable of handing higher call and order volume. They wrote new employee manuals, created new forms, and established streamlined procedures for handling orders. Thirteen years after that nightmarish Christmas, they are still around.

The point of that story is that taking every customer who walks in your door can be very troublesome. Most entrepreneurs find that it's a good idea to exercise more discretion in selecting who you will serve. On my bulletin board is an index card with the following admonition:

I will take no opportunities that cannot offer:

1. $75 per hour, net of research costs,
2. Rates of at least $1 a word for articles or $.25 for books,
3. $5,000 or more in potential annual sales,
4. $1,000 or higher fees per article assignment,
5. Significant potential for growth,
6. Chances to write about business, technology, investing, or sports, and
7. Clients who are easy to work with.

When I am considering an offer of an assignment or thinking of proposing an article or other project to an editor I've never worked with before, I take a look at these requirements and ask myself whether there is any chance that they will all be fulfilled if this proposal works out. Quite often, I decide that they can't, and I opt not to pursue the opportunity. It's still tempting to take everything I'm offered, however, and I sometimes give in.

Even after many years of constantly having a backlog, I still wonder whether I may run out of work. I often convince myself that a small or struggling publication that offers low rates may somehow transform itself into a prosperous organization paying top dollar. I think that a low- or no-paying chance to work on an interesting health topic or to begin reviewing books in a field outside my core areas, may make it worthwhile to venture beyond the areas where I am comfortable. Sometimes, despite the fact that other freelancers tell me an editor is hard to work with or a publication is slow to pay, I elect to take a chance that it will be different with me.

Very often indeed, I come to regret taking on the exceptional clients—exceptional because I am granting them an exception to the rules in accepting their business. The pay never goes up, the editor never gets a new attitude, the new field proves to be uninteresting. Don't get me wrong. I'm not an arrogant vendor who expects customers to grovel for the chance to do business with me. I have, however, tried it the other way. Several years ago, I lost my temper during a telephone conversation with an editor and told her in a loud voice to "lose my phone number!" before slamming the receiver down. It worked—I never heard from that publication again—but I instantly regretted my actions, recognized them as childish and unproductive, and have never repeated them, or anything like them. That doesn't mean I keep working with people who I deem to be more trouble than they are worth. It just means that I treat them with respect.

People I don't want to work with have every right to be in business and they may very well be perfectly fine for others to work with. I've just learned what works with me, and I've learned to stick with that if I want my lifestyle venture to work smoothly. And I expect the same sort of behavior from myself that I ask of my customers.

Many small business owners have not learned this lesson. They take on the wrong customers and wonder why things are not going well. Who is the wrong customer? It's anybody who isn't going to provide you with what you need as an entrepreneur to be successful. Common characteristics of a good customer include:

- A need for the precise services and products you are best positioned to provide,
- The ability and willingness to pay what you need to charge,
- An inclination to say what they want, and
- A sense of obligation to want what they said they wanted.

Some entrepreneurs might leave out the last two, figuring it's up to you to learn how to satisfy the customer. There's some validity in that, but when you're a lifestyle entrepreneur, you are probably running a small enterprise where any time spent decoding mysterious needs or catering to elusive expectations is likely to come straight out of your own day.

You could add many more qualifications, such as "located in the Tri-Valley area" or "able to refer me to some exciting new opportunities." It all depends on what you want. That brings up the next topic: knowing yourself.

Knowing Yourself

Know thyself, said Aristotle, and he might have been speaking directly to lifestyle entrepreneurs. One of the most valuable assets you can have as a lifestyle business owner is to know exactly what you want from the enterprise and what you have to provide both to it and to your customers. This is not necessarily as easy as it sounds. You may not realize that you hate working with the public until you spend a few weeks on your feet behind a counter taking orders in the pizza restaurant you have started. You may assume that you'll love working at home alone, until you start getting depressed and anxious because there's no one around to talk to.

You don't have to wait until you're in over your head before knowing what you should have done. Make an effort in advance to figure out the people and arrangements you will enjoy working with, and try to set those up, while avoiding conflicting circumstances. Ask yourself the following questions, and use the answers to help determine the best arrangement with regard to the people you will work with as a lifestyle entrepreneur:

- Do you enjoy meeting and working with a lot of new people, or are you more comfortable sticking with a small group over a long period?
- What do you do well?
- What would you like to do well?
- How important is money to you?

- How important is it for you to feel that you are constantly developing your skills?
- Do you only feel comfortable if you are working at the highest level? Or do you prefer a less-challenging environment?
- How well do you take criticism?
- Do you enjoy working in arrangements where all the details are spelled out in written form, or do you prefer working on a handshake?
- Are you comfortable working with people you've never met face to face?
- Do you enjoy being held to high standards and meeting them?
- Do you like supervising other people, or would you prefer to do the work yourself if possible?

It is probably impossible to know exactly what you want before you try it out. Still, if you go into lifestyle entrepreneurship with as much information as possible about the kind of people you want to work with, you'll increase the odds of setting up a situation you'll be happy with.

NINE

Taming Technology

Without a high-speed internet connection, Mark Abouzeid wouldn't be able to run an information technology consulting venture from a century-old villa in Italy. Without the ability to set up her own e-commerce site on the World Wide Web, Darcy Volden Miller wouldn't be able to operate an on-line gift registry from her Austin, Texas, lakeside home.

So why do these lifestyle entrepreneurs say things like this:

Darcy: "It is getting really hard. I had to turn my telephone ringer off because it's been ringing off the hook from these women wanting to sign up."

Mark: "While I may take my laptop upstairs to work on something, that's as far as it goes. I have a cell phone but it's not used a lot."

These lifestyle entrepreneurs have a love-hate relationship with technology. On the one hand, it makes their lifestyles possible. "Thanks to the internet, two ISDN lines, and a satellite dish, I can live in a small village of 250 people surrounded by olive trees and wake to Michelangelo skies everyday," rhapsodizes Mark, whose former career was as a workaholic investment banker. Echoes Darcy: "I love being here at our little house on the lake and pounding away on my computer with this view."

Although it may sound as though these lifestyle business owners are unusually confused, actually they're just reflecting the attitudes of society in general. One survey of Americans found 35 percent of respondents identified the pace of technological change as a major threat to the country.[1] In another survey by the group, only 13 percent said technology had made their lives better than their perception of life in the 1950s. The same organization found twenty-two out of 100 people feel cellular phones have made life worse.

One concept rises clearly above all this confusion: Technology can help you as a lifestyle entrepreneur, or it can hurt you. Successful lifestyle entrepreneurs have to learn how to harness technology to their own uses, while taming it so that it doesn't damage the very lifestyle they are pursuing.

How Technology Can Help

I received my initial exposure to computers in the late 1970s, first in a woeful experience taking a Fortran programming class that used punch cards and then at a newspaper using more up-to-date terminals connected to a minicomputer. I purchased my first desktop computer in 1983 and at the same time bought one of the first laptop computers, a Radio Shack Model 100. For many years I carried that Model 100 around in my briefcase, taking notes for interviews and writing articles on it in all kinds of situations. In many ways, it was an important part of my eventual move to become a full-time lifestyle entrepreneur. Having my own computer in my briefcase enabled me to work on freelance articles during my lunch hour, helping me to develop the business contacts I'd need when I severed the employment umbilical cord. Eventually, I wrote regularly for *PC World* and other technology magazines, reviewing computer software and systems, and even wrote a book, *Mastering Home Networking* (Sybex, 2000), on the once-arcane concept of connecting home computers into a network.

I am a fan of information technology. I am always on the lookout for a new piece of software, a new gadget, or a new information service that will help me to do more with less effort and greater enjoyment. By and large, I believe my lifestyle has benefited enormously from the investment I have made in learning to use information technologies. Certainly, the thought of going back to a typewriter for writing and a rotary dial phone and snail mail for communication is not a pleasant one. Assuming you agree with that, and are willing to learn some new tricks to help your lifestyle venture succeed, here are some considerations about how to employ technology as an assistant in that effort.

Technologies You Are likely to Employ

It's hard to imagine running a business without computers today. As far back as 1992, a study of small business owners by two Western Carolina University professors found that 100 percent used some kind of computer.[2] That study involved only fifty-three companies in a few southeastern American states. But a much larger study by the U.S. Census Bureau found that by the year 2000, if you didn't use a computer, you were one of a dwindling minority.[3]

The bureau's study also looked at how people used computers and generated findings that conform to my own observations about what computers are good for. The most popular uses, in descending order, were word processing, games, and e-mail. Other communications, including finding news and other information on the internet, was another important activity. E-commerce, including buying tickets and making on-line reservations, was another major activity. Smaller but significant percentages employed computers for analysis, including use of electronic spreadsheets and databases.

What kinds of technology might you be able to use? Here's a list of technologies commonly employed in small business:

- Computers, including desktop, laptop, and handheld computers
- Printers, including laser and inkjet types
- Modems, including analog telephone modems providing conventional internet access and digital modems for high-speed internet service
- Copiers, scanners, digital cameras, and other image-capturing and reproducing devices

- Fax machines
- Answering machines and automated answering services
- Telephones, including multiline systems and telephone headsets
- Computer networking adapters and hubs
- Wireless communications equipment and services, including cellular phones, pagers, cordless telephones, and wireless networking

Odds are you won't need all of these, at least at first and possibly not ever. That's good because you could spend many thousands of dollars equipping even a one-person home-based business with all this technology. Entrepreneurs need to avoid the temptation to get every conceivable piece of equipment before going into business. It's better to make a conservative assessment of what you will need and plan to add on elements as your need for them becomes apparent.

Here's a list of questions you can ask yourself to help you decide what and how much technology you'll need:

- What kind of work will you be doing primarily with your computer? Word processing? Graphics and design? E-mail and using the internet? Others?
- How much time will you be spending at your computer?
- How much time will you spend on the phone? Will you be talking to clients, customers, or others? What kind of image do you want to project to callers who are leaving messages?
- How much time will you spend working away from your main place of business?
- When you are away from your office or other base, meeting with clients or working at remote job sites, how will technology play a role in what you are doing?
- What kind of information do you need access to when you are in your office? Away from your office? Traveling?
- How many pages will you print from your computer printer in a typical day, week, or month? How many pages will you photocopy? Fax?

- How important is the quality of your printouts, copies, and faxes? Do you need to print or copy in color?
- How much will you be using the internet? What will you be using it for? E-mail? Research? If you are transferring files via the internet, how large will they be?
- How large is your office or place of business and what kind of access to telephones, computers, and other technology will you need when away from your desk?
- How much time and talent do you have for mastering the technology you will buy?

After you have thought through some of the answers to these questions, you are ready to begin outlining your technology needs.

The type of work you are doing at your computer is important because computers come in many different levels of power, sophistication, flexibility, and, of course, expense. If you are like many computer users, primarily doing word processing, you probably won't need the latest, fastest computer on the market. I use computers that are five or more years old almost every day (although I also have newer machines) and have no trouble using industry-standard software on them.

The spiral of technological sophistication that has been driving personal computer sales may, in fact, be running out of energy. Personal computer software and hardware has reached such a high level of performance today—and, in fact, for the last several years has been at such a level—that most users no longer need to upgrade machines and programs every year or two. Keep in mind the qualifier "most." People who are doing graphics design, web site development, and some types of intensive database work may require much more powerful machines than the typical user. But if you're just doing word processing and electronic mail—the two most popular uses for computers—you are likely to be quite happy with a machine that is far less than cutting-edge.

It's important to know how much time you will be spending at your computer for a couple of reasons. People who work long hours at a computer screen generally are happier if they have a large display monitor to look at. That's particularly true if you are doing anything that involves graphics. A large monitor with a sharp picture can be very expensive, but it may be worth it if it keeps you from having to squint to make out details.

Your choice of a telephone system will also depend on the time you will spend using it. Many people who spend large amounts of time on the phone prefer to get a cordless phone with a headset. That allows them to move freely while talking on the phone. Your productivity can be a lot higher if you have both hands free to type notes and can walk around to locate files or do other tasks while on the phone. A speakerphone can provide much the same advantages.

Consider also who you will be talking to. If you are discussing private financial matters with sensitive clients, you might be well-advised to avoid cordless phones as well as cellular phones. The fact that these phones broadcast your conversations makes them less secure from eavesdropping than hardwired phones. Wireless and cordless phones do employ security such as encoding messages and hopping among different radio frequencies to foil unauthorized listeners, but even the best defenses are potentially breakable.

You should carefully consider your choice of a method for taking telephone messages. For many entrepreneurs, an inexpensive answering machine works well. Local telephone companies also offer automated answering services that sound and work much like the costly voice mail switchboards used at large companies. Higher-end answering machines can provide the same image to people calling to leave a message, without the monthly fees charged by the phone companies.

The amount of time you will spend working away from your main place of business is a key consideration in selecting technology. For instance, if you spend virtually all your time out of the office, you may not want to invest in a desktop computer. You may be better off buying a full-featured laptop or notebook computer and using that as your primary PC.

The type of work you will be doing while away from your base also matters. Are you meeting with clients? Working at remote job sites?

If you spend most of your day on outside sales calls, a handheld personal digital assistant (PDA) may be a good investment because it keeps a database of contacts and an up-to-date schedule of activities handy.

Next, consider the kind of information you will need access to, both at your main location and while away from the office. For instance, if you need to be able to visit clients out of town and still have access to information that resides on your desktop, you may need to purchase a laptop computer and equip both machines with remote-control software that lets you tap into your desktop database over telephone lines. On the other hand, you may be able to preload the necessary information into a laptop or even a handheld computer or PDA.

The pervasiveness of computers, e-mail, and web sites hasn't reduced the importance of the hard-copy face you present to the world. Before settling on a computer printer, fax machine, or photocopier, you need to come up with an estimate of the quantity and quality of printed materials that will be needed from them in a given span of time. For instance, if you expect to print many thousands of pages during a typical month, you would be well-advised to choose a laser printer for your output. An inkjet printer, the other popular choice, is more costly to operate at higher volumes. Yet the inkjet may be better if you don't require high volumes or you need to print in color—a feature available on low-cost inkjets but still very expensive on laser printers. Similar concerns should be taken into account when you are selecting a fax machine or photocopier.

To a considerable degree, your ability to access information through technology is more important than how powerful your computer is or how fast your printer works. Make an estimate of how much and in what manner you will be using the internet. If you expect to be using it just for occasional short electronic mail messages, then you are well-suited to an inexpensive analog telephone modem and a garden-variety internet service. If, at the opposite extreme, you will spend many hours on-line surfing complex web sites and downloading and uploading large attached files, then a cable or DSL modem and appropriate high-speed internet service will be very helpful.

High-speed service is not available everywhere and is at least two to three times as costly as conventional service, but the increase in performance—as much as twenty times faster—is well worth it to many small businesses.

How large is your office or place of business? Will you need to be able to place and take phone calls when away from your desk? Cordless and cellular phones are ideally suited for allowing you to stay in telephone contact when roaming through a store, a factory, or even a good-sized home-based business. Some entrepreneurs whose businesses occupy acres or square miles, instead of square feet, such as country lodge operators and tour guides, employ low-powered radio transceivers to keep in touch with other workers or the front desk. These devices avoid airtime charges of cell phones while letting you roam much further than you could with a cordless phone.

Will you have several computers in different rooms that need to be able to talk to each other? Home and small-office computer networks are relatively easy to install and offer significant advantages if you have several people in one location who need to share information such as a computerized database of customers, equipment such as an expensive printer, or a service such as a high-speed internet connection. These days, wireless networks are the best choice for many small businesses because of their increasingly simple installation, excellent performance, and rapidly declining cost.

One of the most important questions you need to ask yourself is whether you have the time, talent, and inclination to master a great deal of new technology. Few, if any, business users get all possible benefit from their investments in computers and other information processing gear, simply because the systems are too complicated to fully understand without many hours of study. For every additional piece of software or new gadget you buy, you are increasing the burden of learning and practice you will have to carry out if you are to become proficient with the new system. It's not a bad idea to start with what you know, plus a small amount of what you don't know, and add new technologies as their need becomes apparent.

Balancing Long-term and Short-Term Objectives

The choices you make in selecting technology when you are starting out can either help or hinder you down the road. If you spend too much on technology you don't use, you won't have those funds available for other uses that might prove more beneficial. If you skimp or choose the wrong technology, you may hamstring your ability to operate effectively.

Holly Bolinger had to confront this issue head-on when she was selecting computerized sewing equipment for her custom embroidery company. "We researched different types of embroidery equipment from several different manufacturers," says the Canton, Ohio, entrepreneur. She found a wide range of capabilities and prices to choose from. After narrowing it down to two choices, one representing a less costly option and the other offering more flexibility and capacity at a higher price, they attended a demonstration. The decision was difficult and crucial because they were borrowing the money to purchase the machine and, once they had taken delivery, their choice would greatly influence what kind of business they could do.

"We decided we would rather have the strength and capabilities of the Cadillac of the machines," Holly says. Her research into the technology gave her the confidence to disregard the recommendations of the machine's dealer and purchase additional software that would allow them to design their own embroidery patterns. That, she figured, would enable them to offer distinctive designs, instead of relying on stock embroidery patterns available from suppliers. "This turned out to be an excellent decision and a source of additional cash flow," she says.

The same issues face entrepreneurs selecting any type of technology. The solution to them is to take the same attitude Holly did: Examine the technology from a business perspective, and make sure that the perspective is that of your business. Here are key questions to ask when trying to balance short- and long-term requirements:

- Will purchasing more sophisticated and costly equipment allow me to serve more customers or approach different markets?
- Will having access to this technology have a predictable impact on my business's revenues or profits?
- Will this technology improve my lifestyle?
- Can I cost-effectively upgrade this equipment later on if I find out that I need additional capacity or features?
- Will I be able to use this technology effectively, given my normal level of understanding and energy when it comes to learning new technologies?
- Do I have a specific current or foreseeable need for the features I am purchasing?

The desired answer to all the above questions is yes. If you can't answer any of them positively, reconsider the technology you are about to purchase. After you have spent a few weeks perusing computer magazines or talking to salesmen in electronics stores, it's easy to get starry-eyed over the latest and greatest features. But trade journalists have been known to declare that the new models are vast improvements over the old or some new gadget is a must-have when, in fact, they aren't. And salespeople, even if well-intentioned, don't necessarily know what your business requires. It pays to do your own analysis and come to your own decisions.

For example, for years I had a powerful longing for a handheld computer. I wrote several round-up reviews of handheld computer products and had a chance to experiment with many samples for extended periods of time. The tiny little computers were a lot of fun, but when I sat down and thought about it, I didn't have any real need for one. I do most of my work sitting right at my desk, so I had little need for a portable electronic calendar or contact database. I refrained from buying one, because it didn't serve any business need and I didn't have the several hundred dollars it would have required to purchase one. I eventually received one as a gift and, as I suspected, have enjoyed using it, but have done little with it that I couldn't have done without it.

You can also hamstring yourself by selecting the wrong technology. When I purchased my first desktop computer in 1983, I selected the Model 4 computer manufactured by Radio Shack. I had reasons for this decision. Radio Shack also made the Model 100, the first notebook computer ever sold. I was determined to get one of those and wanted to have a desktop from the same manufacturer so I could be sure the two machines would work well together. They did work well together, and the Model 100 was a very useful tool.

The Model 4 desktop turned out to be a bad selection, however. At the time, IBM-compatible PCs were the dominant design in the marketplace, and the Model 4 was incompatible with it. The Model 100, on the other hand, worked well with other computers. A better solution, then, would have been an IBM-compatible PC along with the Radio Shack portable. But having spent several thousand dollars on the Model 4-based system, it took me several years to convince myself to switch to a PC-compatible desktop.

Being technologically out of step for that long kept me from competing as effectively as I could as a journalist covering the computer industry. That's an example of how the technology you choose can affect your business strategy, for better and for worse.

Taking a Break from Technology

Now it's time to go back to the first point made in this chapter: Having all this technology can be a blessing and a curse. While cell phones are on the whole wonderfully convenient devices, they do pose problems. The sound of a ringing cell phone intruding on your space as you try to rest after a long day of battling transportation systems has led to more than a few of the diminutive communicators being pitched into the nearest body of water and left to rust. Being constantly on call via a wireless device clipped to your belt or purse strap is stress producing. That's why many lifestyle entrepreneurs take vacations from cell phones as well as voice mail, e-mail, and any other kind of communication.

The thought of cutting off contact with your business to take a vacation can be a little worrisome. But if you plan ahead, you should be able to sever the umbilical cord tying you to your responsibilities—at least for a time—without creating a problem.

When Mark Abouzeid had a consulting client who demanded he be available anywhere, anytime, including on holiday, he simply told the client that he never took a cell phone with him on vacation. In reality, he did, since it would have been silly to leave such a helpful object behind. But, as Mark explains, "I don't want to be thinking that my cell phone might ring." By saying he wouldn't be reachable, he encouraged the client to get along without him for a week, and, of course, the client did just fine.

TEN

Growing Without Grief

At many businesses characterized as entrepreneurial, growth is the ultimate goal. Growth in sales, growth in market share, growth in locations, growth in earnings per share—basically, growth of almost everything except debt and losses is considered essentially good. For lifestyle entrepreneurs, that's not necessarily so. Those who are in the early start-up stage generally embrace growth and seek it with a great deal of energy. But more than a few are specifically antigrowth. And many regard growth warily at best.

"I struggle with that a lot," says on-line retail entrepreneur Darcy Volden Miller. Darcy's home-based venture has been far more successful in financial terms than she ever imagined. And she's full of ideas to do more with it than provide small sellers of handmade baby gifts with an on-line retail portal. But to do so is going to mean big changes, especially in the lifestyle component of a venture that she started specifically to stay home with her newborn son.

"I can play in the minor leagues, but bumping up into the major leagues—I don't know about that," Darcy says. "I'm concerned. Can I handle it?"

So far, Darcy has run a one-woman operation. From her experience working for a big corporation, she knows that having employees is going to vastly complicate her life. But she's getting to the point where she may have to hire somebody. She's had to turn her telephone ringer off because of all the business calls coming in. Now she faces turning on all the complexities of running a business, located outside of the home, with employees and many other changes. "It's not an easy decision to handle," she says. "But I'm going to have to handle it because I'm being pushed that way."

Darcy's ambivalent attitude toward growth isn't as misplaced as it might seem for an entrepreneur, even for one whose business isn't primarily designed to address lifestyle needs. The truth is, growth can be dangerous for any business. There are a lot of reasons for this. For instance, it takes different skills to run businesses of different sizes and at different stages in their existence. If your business grows beyond your ability to run it, you may wind up growing right into failure. One hundred employees is the threshold at which many company founders are said to exhaust their management ability. If they are to grow larger without great difficulties, some entrepreneurial experts say, these founders should hire professional managers to take over many of the senior jobs, possibly even including the CEO's post.

Growth is a potentially serious problem even if you do have the management skills. The story of Penny McConnell provides an example. Penny owned an eight-person bakery in Austin, Texas, where she supplied local retailers with fresh-baked cookies and pastries. One day she dropped by the headquarters of Southwest Airlines in Dallas with samples of a new product, Penny's Pride packaged cookies, and a suggestion that the airline start serving the treats to its passengers. Amazingly, not long afterward, a Southwest buyer called and said the airline wanted to put Penny's Pride on all its flights. The first month's order amounted to a year's worth of sales.

So far, so good. It's every entrepreneur's dream—the big break. But as it turned out, the break broke Penny's Pastries. First, Penny had to cut her prices to conform to Southwest's budget. Then she had to borrow heavily to buy new ovens and other equipment, order supplies, hire employees, and lease a new kitchen. Even then, all might have been well, but she experienced technical problems trying to modify her fresh-baked recipes and packaging in order to provide shelf-stable cookies. Costs took off like a Boeing 737 out of Dallas Love Field. The anticipated profits vanished and soon losses took their place. Six months after shipping Southwest's first order, Penny's Pastries sought protection from creditors under the bankruptcy laws.

Penny McConnell is a smart woman, and Penny's Pastries was a viable company. The only thing they really did wrong was to grow too fast. It's a very common scenario. When you grow so fast that you don't have enough cash on hand to pay for everything it takes to grow—new equipment, new facilities, more supplies and inventory, and more employees—you borrow as much as you can to make it all work. The first time there's a problem, it stops working, and the whole poorly supported apparatus comes crashing down.

As a lifestyle-oriented entrepreneur, this is unlikely to happen to you. I primarily tell this story to legitimize a cautious attitude toward growth. Some people will suggest that you simply must grow and expand in order to stay alive. But growth is actually quite often very dangerous and should be approached with caution. That warning is doubly true when the primary purpose of your business is to provide you with a desirable lifestyle. A fast-growing business is hard to pair with a good lifestyle.

Just Say No

Several years ago, business consultant Janet Drez's Chandler, Arizona, home-based venture was growing rapidly. "I had two employees working for me and things were rocking and rolling," Janet recalls. She toyed with the idea of moving out of her home and into a rented office. She even went to look at commercial space with a real estate broker. "Then I had one of those 'ah-ha' moments," Janet reports. She asked herself, "'What am I doing? I started this business to be with my children and be involved in their lives, not to be pulled away into another corporate situation.'" Janet put the brakes on her planned move and decided to shrink the business in order to stay home. "I willingly gave up the idea of having my name on the side of a building," she says, "in order to remain focused on what's really important to me—my family."

"Just Say No" has not turned out to be a very good antidrug message, and, while it's a catchy reminder that lifestyle entrepreneurs don't have to take every growth opportunity, I don't think it describes a particularly good way to actually turn down growth. When you simply turn away a customer without any elaboration, you do more than constrain growth. You often create what might be called an anti-customer. This is someone who may have been offended by a curt refusal. If that happens, they may never call or come by again, even at some later date when you need the business. They won't give you any good referrals to customers who might be more like what you have in mind. They may even be so put off that they'll work to damage your reputation.

These risks are why I rarely if ever just say no. Instead, I thank the prospect for offering me the business. I explain why I can't take the job. I ask them to think of me again if they have an opportunity that fits what I do. I promise to contact them if my circumstances change and I feel we would be a better fit at some future date. Finally, I offer to refer them to someone who would be a good fit for this job. Taking this attitude reassures customers that their need is legitimate and that it ought to be filled by someone, even if that someone is not me.

As a rule, if you can't fulfill someone's request the first time they contact you, you'll never hear from them again. But when you offer referrals and explain why you can't do the work, at least you reduce the chances you'll make an enemy by trying to restrain your own growth.

Avoiding Stagnation

Now that I've thoroughly dissed the "growth is necessary" viewpoint, it's time to admit that there is something to be said for growth. It just depends on what you mean by growth. A company needs to increase its revenues and cash flow or profits by at least as much as the inflation rate, or it's actually losing ground economically. In the same way, an entrepreneur whose salary doesn't increase over the long haul by as much or more as the Consumer Price Index is effectively taking a cut in pay. There's nothing wrong with making less and enjoying it more, of course. This concept underlies the basic idea of the lifestyle entrepreneur. It's when you are making more and enjoying it less that you have look askance at growth and wonder whether that is the direction you should go.

Don't forget that there is more than one kind of growth. Even if revenues remain stagnant, a lifestyle entrepreneur who tries out new ideas, learns new skills, makes new contacts, and explores new horizons is growing. This sounds a trifle sappy, even to me. But I believe one of the great things about being a lifestyle entrepreneur is that you are free to try to move your business in any direction in which you want to go, for whatever reason is important to you. You don't have to follow the market or the public taste or orders from on high. If you want to try to do business in a certain way, you are free to give it a shot.

It's almost embarrassing to recount the many arenas in which I have attempted to compete as a lifestyle entrepreneur. I have made serious forays into newsletter publishing and teaching seminars. These were ventures that showed promise, generating enough income to cover their costs and provide for a small profit. After trying them out for a while, though, I decided that wasn't the way I wanted to go, so I dropped them. I might well have grown my business much larger by now if I'd stuck with the newsletters or seminars. They were and are viable businesses, and I seemed to have what it took to make them work. But by trying and giving them up, I profited in another, perhaps more important way. I learned something about another business and about myself. I met some interesting people and tried some interesting things. I reassured myself, once again, that what I'm doing is probably the best thing for me to be doing. This is the kind of growth that appeals to lifestyle entrepreneurs as much or more than the kind of growth that appeals to venture capitalists. And I'm far from alone in that assessment.

Charlotte Schmickle is something of an expert on the topic. She was director of the Center for Personal Growth at Guilford College in Piedmont, North Carolina, when she and her husband, Bill, a professor and chairman of the political science department there, decided to leave the college and run the Flag House Inn B&B in Annapolis, Maryland. "We decided, once our children were either in or about to go off to college, to look for a place with less grass to mow (we had had six acres), a town with the ability to get out and walk around, a town with more cultural life close at hand, and if we ended up near the water, that would be great too," explains Charlotte. "So, here we are in Annapolis, owning and operating a successful B&B and loving every minute."

That's not the kind of growth that will get you into the *Inc. 500*, but it will give you a feeling of satisfaction that mere accumulation of money might not.

Serial Lifestyle Entrepreneurs

There is a distinct subset of entrepreneurs who, although they are constantly and actively seeking growth, do not want to run large companies. These entrepreneurs get a personal thrill from starting companies and building them until they are self-sufficient. But then, just as things are starting to go really well, they sell the company and move on to start another one. Are these lifestyle entrepreneurs? I would argue that they are, since they are starting their companies for other than financial reasons. They just like starting companies.

Earlier I introduced you to Harry Gruber, the San Diego medical doctor, inventor, and entrepreneur who has founded five separate ventures. His first was a biotech research firm that spawned two additional businesses, both in biotech. His latest, at this writing, is an on-line fund-raising enterprise launched in 1999. His biggest financial success was an internet video and audio delivery company that sold for an outlandish sum at the height of dot-com mania. But all of Harry's companies were quite successful, with three of them even going public. Not surprisingly, Harry has been recognized as a top entrepreneur by a number of organizations. He is also extremely wealthy, and yet he keeps starting more companies. He is a classic serial entrepreneur who is doing it not because he needs to financially, but because he likes to or has some goal in mind—in the latest case, it's contributing a new tool for philanthropy.

Growing Profits, Not Sales

What most people mean when they talk about growth is growth in sales, the top line on the income statement. Emphasizing revenue growth over increasing profit or cash flow is one of the characteristics that small business market researcher John Warrillow uses to distinguish more traditional entrepreneurs, which he called Mountain Climbers, from more lifestyle-oriented entrepreneurs, such as the ones he refers to as Craftspeople. But for a lifestyle entrepreneur, more sales is not what it's about. Even in a strictly financial sense, what's important to a lifestyle entrepreneur is what's left over from sales after all costs are paid.

Can you grow profits without growing sales? Certainly. That's a matter of reducing costs without losing revenues. It can be difficult and complex to cut costs without sacrificing revenues. Large companies employ battalions of cost accountants, marketing experts, and manufacturing engineers in order to find and remove costs that don't help to increase sales. With a lifestyle entrepreneur, it is often much simpler, however. The major cost in many lifestyle ventures is paying the owner. If you can reduce the amount of time you spend performing a task that generates a given amount of revenue, you can increase profits without growing sales.

Here's a straightforward example. In a typical year, I complete approximately 100 writing projects, ranging from full-length books to brief articles of a paragraph or two. Starting a new project involves, at minimum, setting up a file folder or two, creating a new computer directory, and doing a little paperwork. When each of these projects is completed, I make out an invoice and perform some bookkeeping entries in Quicken. When the check arrives, I make a few more bookkeeping entries and take the check to the bank to deposit it. All this administrative work adds up to approximately one hour of time per project. That's 100 hours per year spent on paperwork. To consider what this means, imagine if I could get a single project that provided enough work and income to sustain me for an entire year. If I had to issue only one invoice and do all the other things just once, that would free up ninety-nine hours a year. I could take almost two and a half weeks off, at forty hours a week, and still earn the same income.

Realistically, a 99 percent reduction in paperwork isn't going to happen. But for every couple of small opportunities I turn down and replace with a single larger project, I save, on average, about an hour. It is realistic to think this could happen with, say, 25 percent of the projects I work on. Reducing the number of projects from 100 to seventy-five would give me half a week's vacation annually with no sacrifice in earnings.

Paperwork reduction is a simple, commonly applicable example. But there are many other ways to increase your profit without increasing sales. This may involve anything from cutting costs by buying office supplies in bulk to changing the direction of your business. Cheryl Leonhardt left banking and began her career as a lifestyle entrepreneur by starting a golf association for women in business. She went from that to writing a book, *Breaking the Grass Ceiling: A Woman's Guide to Golf for Business* (Triumph Books, 1998), to doing consulting engagements for corporations, to, now, giving speeches and conducting seminars. "I'm trying to position myself as America's Business Golf Coach," says Cheryl.

As a result of changing her basic strategic direction, both her business and her lifestyle have improved. She gives two dozen or so presentations a year, charging up to $8,000 for a keynote presentation. "It's a heck of a lot nicer making your annual salary with twenty or thirty speeches and seminars than going in every single day and slugging it out," notes Cheryl. "And I'm still working out of my house, which is wonderful. It gives me time to get to the driving range and work on my game and still get to the airport and go to the next speaking assignment."

Measuring What Matters

Growth decisions shouldn't be made reactively. You need to fit your decisions about whether or not to go after a new account, new market, or new business into a strategic plan. If you don't, you risk going off in a different direction from the one you intended, and it may turn out to be difficult to find your way back. This is something that many lifestyle entrepreneurs intuitively understand when they think about growth.

"I would like to expand," says special-needs student educator Michelle Paster. "I would like to publish books under the name Learningworks—things like test-taking guides, specific strategy books for kids with learning difficulties. And I do see more than one location." But Michelle isn't willing to put growth at the top of her list of issues. "Quality control is my big concern," she says. "So when I do expand, it will take finding people who have the same ideas and philosophy about education and have good relations with the kids."

If you are going to grow without grief, you have to know what you want to have more of, what you want to have less of, and how much you have of each. If you fail to shape your reaction in terms of your strategy, you are likely to wind up as I did a couple of years ago. I began working for an on-line news service, filing one or more short articles every day. I was blinded by what I saw as the potential to get 25 percent of my annual billings from a single client covering the same set of business topics every day. Furthermore, the early morning deadline for filing the brief write-ups meant I'd have the rest of the day free to work on other material. I already knew that increasing the number of projects I was working on (as opposed to the size of the projects) was not the best way for me to pursue growth without grief. And I already knew that I was tied up many mornings driving in my daughter's school carpool. Yet it took a couple of months of finding that the short write-ups took much longer than I'd planned before I decided to drop this client.

If I'd paid careful attention to what mattered, I would never have taken on the task. One thing that mattered was making time to devote to my parental duties. I was thinking I'd pass this job onto someone else, such as my wife or our in-home child-care provider. But that wasn't what I really wanted (or what they wanted). I was also thinking that making more money was more important than writing about a variety of interesting things or having the opportunity to write at greater length. The experiment wasn't a complete failure, however. It taught me a little more about what's important and how to pay attention to it. That knowledge has enabled me to let several other potential distractions pass by without engaging my energy.

What gets measured, gets managed, according to a saying attributed to Peter Drucker. That means if you measure your monthly sales volume, then activities most likely to affect that number are the most likely to get the most attention. That makes good sense at companies where reports and benchmarks and quotas are big. But as a lifestyle entrepreneur, should you actually measure something? Isn't measurement for the corporate bean counters and efficiency experts? Actually, measurement is important in the smallest companies. Even in my one-person enterprise, I carefully track several variables to help me stay on top of what is happening and, even more important, what is likely to happen down the road. Here are important variables you may want to track to make sure that your growth is on track with your overall strategy:

- cash
- receivables
- sales backlog
- sales performance
- sales forecast
- debt

The item entrepreneurs tend to watch most closely is the amount of cash they have on hand, in the form of checking and money market balances, cash in the till, or other spendable assets. For me, this is simply the amount of cash in our family's checking account and money market account. Every morning, I open a spreadsheet containing our cash flow plan or budget for the next three months. I add any expenditures that have been made or planned since the previous morning and update the current cash balance. I also add any payments that can be expected to arrive thanks to the completion of a job or from some other source. What this tells me is how much cash I have on hand to meet this month's bills, what those bills are likely to be, and how much cash I'll get between now and the end of the month to pay them. With somewhat less accuracy, I can tell how much cash I'll have on hand at the end of next month and the month after that. I become dispirited when there is not enough money in our accounts to pay the bills, and I avoid it by tracking cash closely. If your cash-tracking shows up frequent or serious shortfalls, you may need to grow your revenues or, perhaps, cut costs enough to boost cash generation.

Receivables is another key item for tracking. I enter all my invoices into Quicken so that I can easily create a report showing the date, number, payee, amount, and total of all outstanding invoices. This report is used when I work on our cash plan, which I create in Microsoft Excel. I know how fast each of my clients is likely to pay an outstanding invoice, so I can enter in the cash plan the approximate date I can expect a given check to arrive. The total at the bottom of the outstanding invoices is also of great interest. Since it takes about six weeks for the typical client to pay an invoice, I know that I need to have an amount of outstanding invoices equal to approximately six weeks' worth of expenses. Anything less is a call to complete something and get an invoice in the mail. Receivables tracking lets you know whether the rate at which you are generating invoices is fast enough to pay your near-term cash needs. If you can't generate enough invoices to cover those needs, you may need to reduce the amount of time it takes to get paid. You may be able to do this by negotiating with your customers or by reducing the amount of time it takes you to generate a bill. Or you may have to grow your business until your billings reach the required level.

Debt is at near-record levels at the moment, for both corporations and individuals. Credit card debt, for instance, is an issue for my growing family. We periodically let our revolving credit balances grow uncomfortably large, and then have to institute a careful management plan to pay them off. When this happens, I track progress on our goal of getting the cards paid off with a graph generated by Quicken. Seeing the stairsteps of a debt reduction graph going in the right direction is a powerful inducement to carry the task to completion. Businesses have to watch debt closely as well. It's especially important to keep in mind any large, nonrecurring debt payments, such as balloon payments on loans. If your business isn't generating enough cash to pay for your debts, you may need to grow. On the other hand, it can be easy to take on too much debt in pursuit of growth. Balance forecast debt payments with forecast cash generation to find out whether borrowing to finance growth will lead to disaster or relief.

Taped to my computer monitor is a small piece of paper with all my current assignments on it. Each entry gives the purchaser, due date, amount, and topic of the job, along with a unique project number and, sometimes, notes such as "contract pending." This is my version of a sales backlog report, something of great interest to every business. Sales is the first input into a company's income statement. Without sales, there will be no money to cover costs and no profits left at the end. If sales backlog falls below a certain level, I know it's time to begin preparing and pitching proposals for articles, books, and other writing projects to my clients and to new prospects.

You can increase your sales backlog by implementing a new marketing campaign, offering existing customers a discount, adding additional salespeople, and many other means. There is a strategic risk to pursuing increased backlog. That is, if your backlog gets too high, you will have trouble filling orders, and customers may become impatient and go somewhere else. Once they leave, they're hard to get back. Make sure that your short-term moves take into account your long-term strategy, and take care that you don't pursue increased sales backlog at the expense of adequate levels of service.

My responsibilities seem to grow every year as my children get older and take up new and sometimes fairly costly activities, especially as the amounts required for education, housing, savings, medical care, and other essentials increase steadily. I have to make more money each year if our financial situation is not to deteriorate. For that reason, I track my billings—the dollar amount of the invoices I have sent out— both year-to-date and over the last twelve months. Using a built-in report created by Quicken, I compare these amounts to the year before. This simple report tells me in an instant whether things are looking up or down over the recent, intermediate-term past and suggests, among other things, what my tax liability is likely to be compared to last year and whether the new things I'm trying this year are, on average, helping or hurting the cause. Comparison reports are a good way for you to see if your venture is making progress financially.

The future is probably more interesting than the past, so I have one more report that gives my projected billings for the current year. To make this, I have an Excel spreadsheet that takes my billings for the year-to-date, divides them by the number of weeks in the year-to-date, and then multiplies by fifty-two. It also shows my weekly average earnings and displays a graph showing how the annual projection has varied over the course of the year. This report is vital in letting me know whether I'm on track to do better than last year or whether I need to turn up the heat.

Managing Measurement

This may sound like an awful lot of tracking for a one-person business where, to be sure, all this information has already entered my head once at least. But I have found that, indeed, what gets measured gets managed, and so I try to track what I think are important measures of my business's activity. Not everything gets tracked everyday. Many things are only measured when some event occurs, such as a payment being received or an invoice being issued. Other measurements are made only sporadically, such as an analysis of the number of hours required to complete certain types of jobs. That is important information, to be sure. But there is such a thing as too much measuring.

In many companies, especially large companies, measurement has taken on a life of its own. People compile quarterly, semiannual, and annual budgets and reports and forecasts without understanding why the measurements are necessary. The measurements themselves are often not used for any vital purpose, although they may have been at one time. If I were to take the time to track the hours invested in every single writing project, it would be a major project in itself. By only doing it every now and then, I manage the number of hours I invest in measuring and increase the payback when I do engage in a tracking effort. By keeping an eye on the measurements as well as on the results of the measurements, I hope that they will be kept healthy and that my lifestyle will too.

Don't forget the unique measurements that no one but you cares about or even knows about. Dave Jacobs, the Houston lifestyle entrepreneur who will only do business with in-state clients, is a good example of someone who uses an idiosyncratic measurement to keep his strategy on track and avoid reactive growth that might damage his vision. This particular parameter is based on geography.

"We do business only in Texas," Dave says. "We crafted a vision, and we've worked hard to stay true to that. It's been hard. We have one big client that's been challenging us to do business outside the state. That's been a tough call. But our vision has been the rudder that's been guiding us. Anytime we have a question about which direction to take, the answer rises to the surface quickly."

Delegate, Delegate, Delegate

Entrepreneurs are famed for being micromanagers who want to make all the decisions, sign everything that needs to be signed, and have their hands in every job in their companies. If you're a one- or two-person operation, there's nothing wrong with that. But when you get much larger, you'll find that some limitations in the ability of humans to manage other humans begins to create problems for you. Back in 1922 a British general named Sir Ian Hamilton suggested that a military leader could directly control no more than six people, tops. Three was better, according to Sir Ian, who based his conclusions on studies of military leaders. The idea took hold, and since then a number of analyses of a manager's effective span of control have suggested that, generally, a manager should directly supervise no more than five people. Again, according to fans of "span of control" theory, that's the maximum. If the people you are supervising are in frequent direct contact, the theory says, you might be able to oversee no more than three people with the same amount of effort.

Not everybody agrees with these conclusions. Certainly in the delayering of business that occurred in the 1990s, many big companies whittled away whole layers of middle management. Sometimes those who remained were directly in charge of ten, twenty, thirty, or more people, with no pronounced negative effect on the company or the surviving managers. But there is strong evidence nonetheless that there are limits to how many people you can personally manage. And when it comes to lifestyle entrepreneurs, these limits are probably even lower than for more conventional businesspeople.

The answer for a lifestyle entrepreneur who wants to pursue growth without sacrificing quality of life is to delegate. Simply put, you can't be like that traditional micromanaging company founder. You have to let other people make some of the decisions that need to be made, so that you don't have to. Otherwise, you'll find that as your business grows, your life shrinks. That seems obvious, but delegation is still hard for many people to do. That may not have to do with any failing of entrepreneurs as much as it has to do with the nature of delegation. It's not as easy as it sounds.

One problem with delegation is that it's misunderstood. It's not the same as giving someone orders. Delegation isn't getting someone else to do your work. What it is, is giving other people the right to do the work they think needs to be done in the manner in which they think it needs to be done. It's not telling someone to fill an order of a certain size for a certain customer and to be sure and have it shipped by 5 P.M. It's putting someone in charge of filling orders and not checking to see that they have done it correctly.

Another problem with delegation is that it requires considerably more effort than it sounds. You have to find, recruit, and hire the right people to delegate to. You have to train them to make the decisions that have to be made. You have to absorb the cost of the mistakes they certainly will make. And you have to control your desire to step in and take over. But when you can find the right people and delegate the right duties, you can have both a sizable, growing business and the lifestyle of a true lifestyle entrepreneur. That's especially true of very small companies, when the addition of a single talented, well-placed employee can cause sales to increase exponentially. But it's also true of more established lifestyle ventures.

Brad Stillahn has twenty employees and $3 million in sales at Denver's Adstick Custom Labels. Yet he works in the office only a handful of hours a week, leaving most details of day-to-day operation up to others. "I just need to keep it under control," he says, "and grow it at a rate that's sufficient to stay under control."

ELEVEN

Ending Well

When you start a business, whether it's a lifestyle business or some other kind, only one thing is certain. You don't know whether it will be successful at providing for your needs—whether it will fail utterly or triumph amazingly. The only thing you know for certain is that, someday, you will leave that business. You will sell it, close it, transfer it to a spouse or child or other relative, pass it on to employees, give your share to other owners, or perhaps pass on yourself someday, still running your business all the way to the end.

This probably doesn't sound like shocking news. But few entrepreneurs have taken it into account in planning for their businesses. According to a U.S. Trust survey reported by Mike Cohn, a family business consultant, in *Keep or Sell Your Business* (Dearborn, 2001), only 36 percent of affluent business owners had a fully developed succession plan. The people surveyed were well-heeled, with a minimum net worth of $3 million and annual income of at least $200,000, and so presumably were pretty sophisticated as well. I don't know of any surveys showing how many lifestyle entrepreneurs have planned for exiting their businesses, but I think it's safe to say that many of them haven't thought it out carefully.

That's a shame, because a lifestyle venture doesn't have to end or stop being valuable just because the person who founded it is no longer involved in it. A lifestyle enterprise can provide a life-enhancing opportunity for spouses, children, siblings, or other family members long after the original owner has gone on to other things. Lifestyle businesses can also create substantial financial value that can be tapped by selling the business, merging it with another firm, or closing the company down and selling its assets. You can even hire a professional manager to run the company after you have left it, paying the manager out of the profits and perhaps leaving enough for you and your heirs to enjoy a comfortable income as well.

The catch to all this is that it's not likely to happen without a good bit of planning and some up-front work. Just to mention one potential obstacle, the same U.S. Trust survey reported that on average the respondents expected to lose 24 percent of their estates to estate taxes. That guess probably understates the rate of estate taxation by around half, however, according to U.S. Trust's figures. You can manage estate taxes with careful planning, but if you fail to plan, you'd better plan to pay. And this is just one problem with ending well. Many business owners assume—wrongly—their offspring will be happy and able to conduct their enterprises after they have retired. Many more assume that their businesses are worth far more to a potential buyer than the market value actually dictates.

If you want your lifestyle venture to end well—and it can—then you need to take these issues into account and start working to overcome them long before the actual day of your transition arrives.

Planning for Retirement

Lifestyle entrepreneurs have the same retirement needs as anybody. You should plan to continue receiving something like 75 percent of your preretirement income after you've mustered out of the workforce if you plan to continue living in the same style. That number is variable, depending on your plans for postretirement travel, whether you will still have children in college, etc. But 75 percent is a good figure to start working with. Where is that income going to come from? Savings, investments, Social Security, and pensions are the answers for most people.

But lifestyle entrepreneurs have to have different answers, for the most part. They may have their savings locked up in their businesses, which may also represent their only significant financial investment. Not having worked as an employee, they can't expect a pension. And if, as some lifestyle entrepreneurs do, they have relatively small incomes from their lifestyle ventures—taking the rest of the value in lifestyle benefits, of course—then they may not have paid as much into the Social Security system as a comparable lifelong employee. That means smaller Social Security payments after retirement.

So is there any hope for the lifestyle entrepreneur who longs for a comfortable retirement or wants to have something to pass on to the next generation? Indeed there is. Setting up your post-entrepreneurial life isn't as straightforward as punching a clock for forty years and settling back to collect pension checks. But it is well within the competency of anybody who can start and run a successful business, as long as you realize that, as with so many other aspects of business ownership, it's up to you to make it work. You are completely responsible for funding your own retirement.

Fortunately, there are a number of attractive savings options for U.S. entrepreneurs. The Internal Revenue Service allows the creation of several tax-advantaged accounts that let you get most of the same benefits as an employer does when it sets up a pension plan. These go by strange names—SEPs, Keoghs, and IRAs are a couple of the most popular—but their effects are decidedly down-to-earth. Regular contributions to a tax-advantaged retirement savings plan will allow your retirement to be just as secure, if not more so, as an employee of a big company. Other countries have their own tax-advantaged savings programs, including Canada's Registered Retirement Savings Plans and the United Kingdom's Personal Equity Plans.

And, as a business owner, you do have one major opportunity for building wealth that employees do not: your company.

Cashing Out

Although you may profitably operate your lifestyle venture for decades, the biggest and best benefit may not occur until you are ready to leave it. A going business can have a lot of financial value that you can tap by selling it when you are ready to leave. "To some extent that's where innkeepers make their money," says Park City, Utah, lodgekeeper Hugh Daniels. "You really tend to get your return when you sell."

How much of a return can you expect? According to 1997 figures compiled by the Arthur Andersen Center for Family Business (and cited in Cohn's *Keep or Sell Your Business)*, a small, closely held business was likely to be sold at a price ranging from six to nine times the company's earnings before taxes and interest charges. That number is at the high end of historical ranges and is likely to fluctuate with general economic trends, going down when times are bad and up when times are good. It will also vary by industry as well as by individual company. To find out what your business is likely to be worth, check with an industry association, talk with a business broker, or have an appraisal performed. On-line information provider BizStats.com also has a useful list of rules of thumb for valuing specific types of businesses. Of course, you can only know for sure what a business is worth when you find a buyer. But the point is, you may have a lot of financial strength in your company that you can use to fund a comfortable life after you retire.

Selling your lifestyle business for a nice sum of money can be a satisfying way to end an endeavor that has provided you with a lot of enjoyment. After thirteen years of running the Old Miner's Inn, Hugh Daniels and his wife were beginning to lose their enthusiasm. "How much longer can we do this?" Hugh wondered. "Should we think about selling now versus waiting until we're really tired of things and aren't as up and happy about taking care of guests?"

It seemed likely they would be able to find a buyer. From his many years in the industry, his involvement in industry associations, and his work as a consultant to other innkeepers, Hugh knew that inn purchases tend to be impulsive. And there was no shortage of that impulse among visitors to the Old Miner's Inn. "I can't tell you the thousands of guests I've had who said, 'I wish I could do something like this,'" Hugh says.

However, it was a chance comment to a local businessperson that led to a buyer for Old Miner's Inn. "A guy here had bought another inn," Hugh recalls. "In a casual conversation, I said, 'You ought to buy our inn, and I'll run them both for you.' And that's what we did."

Hugh's next move was not, however, to ride off into the sunset with a pocket full of money. Like many sales of small, closely held enterprises, the lodge was sold on an installment plan with Hugh providing the financing and also agreeing to stay on for several years to run it. Part of the reason for that arrangement was the buyer's request to spread out the payment. Part was the buyer's need for a skilled manager who was familiar with the property to run it. And part was Hugh's impetus to protect the value of the business he had built. He knew from watching sales of other inns that new buyers sometimes made changes that alienated established customers and then, when things didn't seem to be working so well, wanted to give the inn back to its previous owners.

Hugh's management contract says he has veto power over all decisions. "If he defaults, I want all the guests to stay," he explains. And with Hugh still on the job while the deal winds to closure, the business remains healthy. "Most guests don't even think we've ever sold," says Hugh. Hugh will continue running the Old Miner's Inn for a few more years. When the time comes for him to leave the inn and turn management over to the new owners, he'll collect a tidy balloon payment to complete the sale. At that point, he and his wife plan to begin a consulting business advising other inn owners. If you're planning to sell your business some day, keep in mind some of the lessons from Hugh's successful transition:

Plan ahead. Consider how you might cash out of your business well before the need arises.

Make your business salable. Keep good financial records and prepare the business to run without you at the helm.

Think about what happens after the sale. Take steps to protect your remaining interest, if any, in the business.

Not every business owner recognizes the need to plan for an exit. One study found that 16.1 percent of family firms said the current CEO would "never" retire.[1] That may be about as unrealistic as you can get. Fortunately, many business owners eventually do understand that they are not immortal. At some point, they begin to explore possibilities for selling the business to the public, to a larger company, or to another entrepreneur who will continue to run it as an independent firm.

One reason for planning ahead is that businesses tend to be illiquid investments. It is difficult to match buyers and sellers and difficult to set values for most of them. It helps if you decide to look into selling your business long before you need to, because the search for a buyer may take years. Furthermore, business brokers tell me that many business owners never actively consider selling their businesses until someone unexpectedly offers to buy it. If you are ready for that proposal when and if it comes, you will be in a much better position to cut a deal you will be happy with.

Making yourself indispensable can be another roadblock for entrepreneurs. It can be flattering to be regarded as indispensable, and many lifestyle entrepreneurs are just that to their businesses. But if you are trying to build a venture that could someday be sold to someone else, then making yourself indispensable isn't a good idea. If the business won't run well without you personally working in it, no one is going to be interested in buying it unless you agree to stay on. So your goal should be to make yourself dispensable. What you want is a business that will run perfectly well without you.

How can you do this? One way is to convert the business from one that is run by intuition and seat-of-the-pants reckoning into one that is based on a system. Written operating guidelines, policy manuals, and the like are essential if you are to provide a means for transferring your knowledge of how to run the business to someone else.

Beyond that, the key word is "sharing," and the two things you have to share are knowledge and power. Brad Stillahn, the owner of Adstick Custom Labels in Denver, is a good example of someone who is willing to give others the authority and information necessary to run many of the company functions without his direct involvement. While Brad is not looking to sell today, when the time comes he will find that his company is much more valuable to a potential owner if it's clear the business will keep doing well without him around.

Selling a business often isn't like selling a used car, where you sign the papers and walk away with no further connection to the item you just sold. Business buyers often pay in installments or company stock. Purchase payments may be dependent on future performance of the company. Quite often, the business owner is asked to stay on for a transition period that may stretch for years. You may wind up working alongside the new proprietor and forced to witness changes that you would rather not see made. Under these circumstances, it pays to think carefully about what happens after the deal is closed. Otherwise, an enterprise that contributed richly to your lifestyle before you sold it may turn out to be a major negative after you sell.

Business ownership is one of the most common pathways to wealth, but it's important not to take wealth-building for granted. Many small businesses turn out not to be sellable when the owner wishes to leave. You have to take definite steps—making yourself dispensable, instituting systems for managing the company, keeping good financial records—if you hope to harvest your dream when the time comes.

Passing It On

The ultimate victory in business or any other sphere is to beat mortality. Lifestyle entrepreneurs may not live longer than other people, but they do have an opportunity to triumph over the Grim Reaper by passing on their self-built enterprises to successors, either offspring or other hand-picked people. Mark Abouzeid and his wife keep their kids' future very much in mind as they work to sustain and develop their lifestyle ventures in Castelmuzio, Italy. "I hope they'll live here," Mark says of the 100-year-old villa where they work and live. "We bought this place with the hope that when they get married and have kids, they'll choose to live here."

Succession planning isn't as easy as setting up a vice presidency for Junior and assuming he or she will slide seamlessly into your place when you decide to leave. One of the biggest limitations is the requirement that the designated successor has to want the job. Experts in intergenerational business planning say that the best way to increase the chances that your child will want to take over your business is to make it seem like a great way to make a living. That means to expose them to the business from an early age. Take your children to work with you or, if work is at home, involve them in it somehow. Have them pack boxes, stuff envelopes, answer the phone, or go on combo business-and-pleasure trips with you. When they're older, pay them a wage to work part-time in the business. Give them a good exposure to all facets of the work. It's also important to make the work seem enjoyable. That means controlling the amount of griping you do and emphasizing the positive benefits.

In the end, however, you can't force anyone to continue the work you have started. Mark Abouzeid has already gotten his arms around that fact and accepted the possibility that their children may not follow in their footsteps. "They can decide for themselves," he says. "But I do hope they won't feel they're trapped into having to do a horrible job."

Twenty years after Gus and Michelle McMahon moved to the Great Smoky Mountains to run a bed-and-breakfast, their youngest daughter, Maqelle, is in line to run the property after they retire. Growing up at Mountain Brook Cottages in Sylva, North Carolina, made her comfortable with the hospitality field, explains Michelle. After working in Atlanta, Fort Lauderdale, and Charlotte, Maqelle returned to the family business with the intention of taking over. It's a move her parents are in accord with.

"Maqelle enjoys the full range of skills needed to run the resort," says Michelle. "She works in the office where her pleasant personality shines when she is on the phone or greeting guests. She has been seen doing roofing, working to clear the nature trail, mowing, or anything her Dad needs help with. He is teaching her the bookkeeping aspects too. The long-range goal is for her to become more and more familiar with the property and how it is run, and by 2005 she will have complete control of the business so that her parents can retire and do more fishing!"

If you don't have offspring who are interested in following in your footsteps, you may be able to find a worthy heir among your employees. John D. Drake has started three businesses, including the international human resources consulting firm Drake Beam Morin. When running

Drake Beam became too time-consuming, he sold it and moved from New York to Maine and started a consulting company. Once again, however, the venture grew large enough to interfere with his other interests. This time, he decided to pass it on to his employees.

"I made a deal with them," John says. "I said I wouldn't take any pay or anything, but I would turn the business over to them for a small percentage of the sales. I gradually let them buy shares, and I gradually withdrew." Now he retains some ownership and derives a small income from his percentage, but isn't actively involved in running the company. "I made myself chairman of the board and used to come in for quarterly meetings," he says. "But I don't even do that anymore."

Nowadays John devotes most of his time to writing, but other lifestyle entrepreneurs are eager to bring more complicated ventures to life after departing their first start-ups. For Utah innkeeper Hugh Daniels, consulting beckons. His many years in the industry and active participation in trade association activities have made him well-known among innkeepers. "I keep reading that I'm an expert," he jokes. "I thought I could make that into a consulting company."

Once again, Hugh is carefully choosing his venture to fit the lifestyle he's after. Most of his consulting customers are innkeepers all over the country. "That will give me the opportunity to do some traveling, as well as choose how much I want to work and not work," he says. "And they're generally in pretty nice places. I have clients in New Hampshire; Lancaster, Pennsylvania; Taos, New Mexico; San Diego; and southern Utah."

The Future of Lifestyle Entrepreneurs

Making the decision to embark on the lifestyle entrepreneurship journey is not an easy or, as a rule, a well-understood one. Jeffrey S. Davis, a management consultant in Needham, Massachusetts, who advises entrepreneurs, is one of the many experienced businesspeople who scoff at the idea of going into business for lifestyle. Such a person, he says, "generally doesn't know what they're getting into. Only for a few is it what they assumed it would be."

Yet as the many business owners interviewed for this book indicate, lifestyle entrepreneurship is a viable option. And it isn't limited to a specific place. In South Africa, the annual entrepreneur awards presented by Business Partners, a South African lender to small and medium-sized companies, have a separate category for lifestyle entrepreneurs. The winner for 2001 was Liyaqat Parker, CEO and cofounder of Foodworld Group, a food retailer that Business Partners cited for its support of social projects in the communities it serves.

In other countries and cultures, lifestyle entrepreneurs are considered the norm, and business owners who are primarily focused on financial gain are looked on as unusual. "In Italy, a lifestyle entrepreneur is almost a given," says Mark Abouzeid. "Americans generally put lifestyle second. Italians put lifestyle first. There are few people who would take a job that put lifestyle second."

Owning a business involves risk and effort, in any culture and at any time. But that's no more true for ventures aimed at improving lifestyle than for those that are purely intended to turn a profit. People may have told Ron Kipp he was striding into madness to leave a good job at a blue-chip company to buy a Caribbean scuba diving resort. In fact, he turned out to be walking into a way of life that almost anyone would find enviable. For a long time, I doubted the value of my own hopes to escape employment and be a lifestyle entrepreneur.

But in both those cases, and in many others, it proved quite possible to mingle a life worth living with a business that supports it. If this book does nothing else, I hope it plants the understanding that entrepreneurship can be more than a painful marathon of overwork and self-denial engaged in for the sake of a doubtful pot of gold at the end. Business ownership doesn't have to be something you trade your existence for. It can truly give you more than just a living. It can give you a life.

Notes

Chapter One

1. From a personal interview with the author, May 1, 2001. Warrillow researches small businesses to provide marketing information to large companies that want to sell products and services to small companies. You can learn more about Warrillow & Co. research at the company's web site, www.warrillow.com.

2. Tom Richman, "The hottest entrepreneur in America," *Inc.* 9 (February 1987): 50. This article describes a category of entrepreneurs with "one overarching distinction: they've all started companies because it was the best way, sometimes the only way, they could get the work they wanted, where they wanted, and on the terms that they wanted." So William Wetzel's suggestion of the term "lifestyle entrepreneur" to describe them is very much in keeping with the way I use it.

3. Hoover's Online, www.hoovers.com, and the Martha Stewart Living Omnimedia web site, www.marthastewart.com.

4. "Forget the Filthy Lucre . . . It's More of a Lifestyle Decision," *The Northern Echo Quarterly Business Review* (August 2001), available at www.echobusiness.co.uk.

5. U.S. Census Bureau, "1992 Characteristics of Business Owners"; survey available at www.census.gov/csd/cbo/.

6. Melinda Henneberger, "Venice Journal; The Gondola Builder, Oddly, Is from the U.S.," *New York Times* (September 14, 2001). Thom Price tells his story there, and he maintains a web site at www.squero.com.

7. This study was cited in Karl Vesper, *New Venture Experience* (Seattle: Vector Books, 1994), a textbook for entrepreneurship courses written by a University of Washington economics professor. The report was originally published in A. C. Cooper, W. C. Dunkleberg, C. Y. Woo, and W. J. Dennis Jr., *New Business in America: The Firms and Their Owners* (Washington, D.C.: The NFIB Foundation, 1990). The actual figure was 23 percent of entrepreneurs reported working under fifty hours a week. It should be noted that another study cited by Vesper, from "Notebook" in *Inc.* magazine for September 1990, showed just 15 percent worked under fifty hours. In both studies, the largest single group, about 30 percent, worked from sixty to sixty-nine hours.

8. This came from an interview I did with Kirkpatrick Sale in July 1999 as part of research for an article, which was never published, about pencils and people who prefer to write with them rather than use word processors.

Chapter Two

1. From a November 11, 1995, press release, "Home-Based Women-Owned Businesses Number and Employ Millions," issued along with the results of the survey. The Center for Women's Business Research is a Washington, D.C., organization that studies the economic and social contributions of women-owned companies.

2. Leonie V. Still and Wendy Timms, "'I Want to Make a Difference': Women Small Business Owners: Their Businesses, Dreams, Lifestyles, and Measures of Success," (paper presented at the meeting of the International Council for Small Business, Brisbane, Australia, June 2000). The full paper, which reported on a series of focus group discussions with sixty-three women small business operators in Western Australia, is available on-line at the web site of the Small Business Advancement National Center of the University of Central Arkansas at www.sbaer.uca.edu/Research/2000/ICSB/.

3. Kitty Cochrane, "Home-Grown Soap Business Thrives," *Natural Life* (March /April 1995); available on-line at http://www.life.ca/nl/42/index.html.

Chapter Three

1. These figures come from *Statistical Abstract of the United States: 2000*, which cites as its source the U.S. Census Bureau publication, *Historical Statistics on Governmental Finances and Employment, and Public Employment, Series GE, No. 1, Annual.* The actual count for 1998, the last year surveyed, is 19,854,000 employees. You can see additional information on the census figures on-line at www.census.gov/govs/www/apes.html.

2. "Currently, small businesses rank labor shortages above taxes and government regulations as their heaviest burden," read a December 1, 1999, news release from the Small Business Administration's Office of Advocacy. The release, headlined "Small Businesses Experiencing a Labor Shortage," announced the results of a study of small business problems regarding finding workers, and the sentence was intended to make the point that, most of the time, government regulations and taxes topped business owners' list of worries.

3. "The Phoenix Forecast: Bankruptcies and Restructurings 2002," prepared by Carter Pate, Managing Partner of Financial Advisory Services of PricewaterhouseCoopers, March 2002. The study predicted about 3,600 of the 11,000 private and public companies it expected to file for bankruptcy in 2002 would obtain court approval of their restructuring plans and continue in business as stand-alone entities or as part of other enterprises.

4. Mark Tatge, "Happy Returns," *Forbes* (October 8, 2001): 224. The article described Nelson Hunt's return to the thoroughbred racing scene and estimated the value of Nelson's trust.

5. "Business Starts and Stops," a November 1999 study co-sponsored by Wells Fargo and the National Federation of Independent Business, a Washington, D.C., small business advocacy group, is drawn from data collected during 1998 by the Gallup Organization in more than 36,000 annual interviews of U.S. households. It covers a variety of elements in the experience of small business creation and termination, including the number of starts and stops, profitability, hours worked, employment, and family involvement. You can look at a variety of information about small business at the NFIB's web site, www.nfib.com.

6. The 2001 Kauffman Center report, "The Growth and Advancement of Entrepreneurship in Higher Education: An Environmental Scan of College Initiatives," referred to a 2000 study by researchers Alberta Charney and Gary D. Libecap that found more than 1,500 colleges offering entrepreneurship courses. It also noted that the number of entrepreneur-training colleges had increased from 400 in 1995 and from just sixteen in 1970.

7. From Mount Royal College's web site description of its Bachelor of Applied Business and Entrepreneurship degree. The full description is on-line at www.mtroyal.ab.ca/Calendar/applied_degrees/BABEpd.htm.

8. Dun & Bradstreet, "IT Business Starts Rising in U.S., Driven by Communications Sector," October 2000. The figures on overall business starts are contained in the report, which is available on-line at www.dnb.com/about/media /press_release/1,,0-223-1012-0-565.html.

9. "Business Starts and Stops."

10. "New Business Starts Attract the 40+ Crowd," *Silicon Valley/San Jose Business Journal* (December 20, 2001).

11. "Attitudes and Behaviors That Create Small Business Success," a November 1999 report from Pitney Bowes that analyzed responses of nearly 2,000 U.S. business owners interviewed by Yankelovich Partners and Pitney Bowes.

12. "20th Annual Small Business Survey Summary Report," Dun & Bradstreet, 2001. Another interesting fact from the report is that 34 percent of owners worked forty hours a week or less. You can see the entire summary report at http://sbs.dnb.com/mktSamples/Small_Business_Survey-Complete _Report.pdf.

13. Edward K. Frank, *The Real World of Small Business* (Galway, NY: Liberty-Grant Publishing Co., 2001). Frank is an experienced entrepreneur, but his estimation of the overall odds of small business failure are too high.

14. Karl Vesper, *New Venture Experience* (Seattle: Vector Books, 1994): 7. Vesper goes into a more detailed analysis of failure studies in *New Venture Strategies,* rev. ed. (Englewood Cliffs, NJ: Prentice-Hall, 1990), but the conclusions are the same.

Chapter Four

1. Marte Sheeran was interviewed by the author in April 1994 for an article, "Dream On," that appeared in the September 1994 issue of *Entrepreneur* magazine.

2. This interview with Tim Smith was conducted by the author in 1995 as part of research for an article on sabbaticals, "Time Out," that appeared in the October 1995 issue of *Entrepreneur*.

3. Interviews with Rich Own and Todd Wichmann were conducted by the author in November 2001 as part of research for an article on reviving old businesses that appeared in the March 2002 issue of *Southwest Airlines Spirit* magazine.

Chapter Five

1. International Franchising Association, "The 20 Most Commonly Asked Questions About Franchising" (Washington, D.C.: IFA, 1996). The IFA cites industry estimates as its sources. You can learn more about franchising at the IFA's web site, www.franchise.org.

2. The Wolf Group case was described in a document titled "Panel Discussion: Franchise Business Opportunities Advertising," moderated by Larry Norton, deputy director at the Federal Trade Commission's Division of Marketing Practices. This transcript is available on the Federal Trade Commission's web site at http://www.ftc.gov/bcp/adcon/adcon2.htm.

3. The McDonald's Corp. describes requirements for its franchisees in "Franchising Frequently Asked Questions" and other documents available on its corporate web site at www.mcdonalds.com.

4. The Bureau of Labor Statistics information was collected in the February 1995 Current Population Survey. It was described and analyzed in Sharon R. Cohany's article, "Workers in Alternative Employment Arrangements" in the October 1996 *Monthly Labor Review*, a government publication. You can see the full article on-line at www.bls.gov/opub/mlr/1996/10/art4exc.htm.

5. Gregory Karp, "Moonlighting Leads to Something Fishy," *The (Allentown, Pa.) Morning Call* (October 1, 2001).

6. "New Data on Multiple Jobholding Available from the CPS," *Monthly Labor Review* (March 1997). A great deal of statistical analysis and information from the CPS is available on-line at www.stats.bls.gov.

Chapter Six

1. Internal Revenue Service, *Business Expenses,* publication 535 (2001); available on-line at www.irs.gov.

2. Steven D. Strauss, *The Big Idea: How Business Innovators Get Great Ideas to Market* (Chicago: Dearborn, 2002), 132.

Chapter Seven

1. I first talked to David Wheeler in December 1997 as part of research for a profile article, "Make My Database," that appeared in the June/July 1998 issue of *Verge* magazine. Since then, I've spoken to David or others at his company several times in order to stay up-to-date on his unusual saga.

Chapter Eight

1. U.S. Census Bureau, "Statistics About Business Size." The document cites as sources published and unpublished data from various surveys the bureau has conducted. You can see details about the census findings on legal organization of businesses on-line at www.census.gov/epcd/www/smallbus.html#Legal.

Chapter Nine

1. Pew Research Center for the People and the Press, "Optimism Reigns: Technology Plays Key Role," October 1999; report is available on-line at www.people-press.org.

2. Small Business Institute Director's Association, "The Under-Utilization of Computerization in Small Business: A Matter of Perspective," January 1992; The survey is available on-line at http://www.sbaer.uca.edu/RESEARCH/1992/SBIDA/92sbi016.htm.

3. U.S. Census Bureau, "Home Computers and Internet Use in the United States," August 2000; available on-line at www.census.gov/prod/2001pubs/p23–207.pdf.

Chapter Eleven

1. Arthur Andersen Center for Family Business, "American Family Business Survey," 1997; available on-line at www.andersen.com.

Appendix: Further Reading

Books About Entrepreneurship

Against All Odds: Ten Entrepreneurs Who Followed Their Hearts and Found Success
By Wendy Harris
John Wiley and Sons, Inc., New York, 2001
A former small business editor at *Black Enterprise* magazine tells how ten African-American entrepreneurs overcame obstacles and learned important lessons on the way to building prosperous businesses.

Big Vision, Small Business: The Four Keys to Finding Success and Satisfaction As a Lifestyle Entrepreneur
By Jamie S. Walters
Ivy Sea Publishing, San Francisco, 2001
This book is one of the first to explicitly address lifestyle entrepreneurship. The central concept is that having a big and growing business is not always better than having a smaller business that allows for a healthy personal life. Jamie Walters's keys address achieving a healthy balance of work and life more than building a strong financial balance sheet.

Downshifting: How to Work Less and Enjoy Life More
By John D. Drake
Berrett-Koehler, San Francisco, 2000
John Drake has started and run big companies and small ones in five decades in business. Here he talks about how limiting your workweek and

using flextime and other tools can keep business from taking the enjoyment out of life.

Entrepreneurial Couples: Making It Work At Work and At Home
By Kathy Marshack
Davies-Black, Palo Alto, Calif., 1998
This psychologist and business consultant shows how couples who start a business together can stay together and maintain equilibrium between demands of business, love, and life.

Free Agent Nation: How America's New Independent Workers Are Transforming the Way We Live
By Daniel H. Pink
Warner Business Books, New York, 2001
Dan Pink's insights into the rise of free agency and his analysis of the trend and its motivations makes good and informative reading for anyone considering whether conventional employment is the only route to a satisfying life.

Guerrilla Marketing: Secrets for Making Big Profits from Your Small Business
By Jay Conrad Levinson
Houghton Mifflin, New York, 1998
This is the third edition of the 1983 book that has become the Bible of low-cost, high-impact marketing for small companies. There are now dozens of titles in Jay Levinson's Guerrilla series on topics from marketing on-line to marketing a home-based business, all based on the idea that you don't have to spend a lot of money to market well.

Guts & Borrowed Money: Straight Talk for Starting and Growing Your Small Business
By Tom Gillis
Bard Press, Austin, Texas, 1997
Tom Gillis is a retired Houston manufacturing company owner whose advice is as firmly tooled as an oil well fitting. Gillis possesses vast expe-

rience and distills it here in a commonsense and well-organized fashion. A useful book for any entrepreneur's shelf.

Honey, I Want to Start My Own Business: A Planning Guide for Couples
By Azriela Jaffe
HarperBusiness, New York, 1997
Azriela Jaffe has degrees in social work and business, is married, and is also an entrepreneur, all of which help explain why she is so good in this book at describing and helping to defuse the stresses that entrepreneurship can bring to an intimate relationship.

Managing by the Numbers: A Complete Guide to Understanding and Using Your Company's Financials
By Chuck Kremer and Ron Rizzuto with John Case
Perseus, Cambridge, Mass., 2000
This book presents a practical approach to preparing and reading financial statements and using them to manage net profit, operating cash flow, and return on assets.

The Mousedriver Chronicles: The True-Life Adventures of Two First-Time Entrepreneurs
By John Lusk and Kyle Harrison
Perseus, Cambridge, Mass., 2001
John Lusk and Kyle Harrison got out of business school at the height of the dot-com craze, and instead of going for the easy money, they decided to start a business to make and market a computer mouse shaped like a golf club. That decision may not have made them millionaires, but their witty and insightful recounting of what did happen makes a good how-to for any entrepreneur.

New Venture Experience
By Karl Vesper
Vector Books, Seattle, 1994
This beefy textbook used to teach entrepreneurial courses contains many case studies, survey results, analyses, and other useful items drawn from

both scholarly and popular publications. I find myself referring to my copy almost anytime I am researching a small-business question.

The Next Level: Essential Strategies for Achieving Breakthrough Growth
By James B. Wood with Larry Rothstein
Perseus, Cambridge, Mass., 1999
All businesses encounter strategic points at which they have to effect major changes if they are to grow to the next level. This book uses a diagnostic tool called Growth Strategy Analysis to show you how your company is doing on key performance variables and provides advice on breaking through to the next stage of growth.

199 Great Home Businesses You Can Start (and Succeed In) for Under $1,000
By Tyler G. Hicks
Prima Publishing, Roseville, Calif., 1999
More than just a list of opportunities that require very little start-up capital, the second edition of this manual shows you how to pick a low-cost business that fits your personality and to successfully start and run it.

Our Wildest Dreams: Women Entrepreneurs Making Money, Having Fun, Doing Good
By Joline Godfrey
HarperBusiness, New York, 1992
Joline Godfrey, a combination of tough-minded entrepreneur and visionary social reformer, defines a new paradigm of business life based on qualities she identifies as belonging especially to women entrepreneurs.

The Portable MBA in Entrepreneurship
By William D. Bygrave
Wiley, New York, 1994
In this encyclopedic reference source, the head of the top-ranked entrepreneurship center at Babson College pulls together a team of small business experts who provide advice on virtually anything relating to being an entrepreneur.

Soul Proprietor: 101 Lessons from a Lifestyle Entrepreneur
By Jane Pollak
Crossing Press, Freedom, Calif., 2001
Artist Jane Pollak exemplifies the lifestyle entrepreneur as well as anybody, and here she provides a detailed, personal recounting of all she has learned in more than a quarter-century of being in the egg-decorating business.

Spare Room Tycoon: Succeeding Independently: The 70 Lessons of Sane Self-Employment
By James Chan
Nicolas Brealey Publishing, London, 2000
A home-based consultant presents seventy lessons of sane self-employment in a warm and often humorous recounting of his struggles to cope with the challenges of lifestyle entrepreneurship.

The Startup Garden: How Growing a Business Grows You
By Tom Ehrenfeld
McGraw-Hill, New York, 2001
Small business journalist Tom Ehrenfeld uses gardening as a metaphor to describe an entrepreneurial approach that never loses sight of the way small business ownership affects your life.

The Stay-at-Home Mom's Guide to Making Money from Home: Choosing the Business That's Right for You Using the Skills and Interests You Already Have
By Liz Folger
Prima Publishing, Roseville, Calif., 2000
The second edition of this step-by-step guide shows women how to start scrapbooking, catering, accounting, and other businesses that let them earn income without leaving home or children behind.

Working from Home: Everything You Need to Know About Living and Working Under the Same Roof
By Paul and Sarah Edwards

Tarcher/Putnam, New York, 1999
This is the fifth edition of the first book by the couple now known as the preeminent experts on home-based business. It's truly an all-in-one reference for home-based business owners, with well-researched and accessible sections on everything from avoiding loneliness to coping with zoning laws.

Other Books

The Future of Success
By Robert Reich
Knopf, New York, 2001
Former U.S. Secretary of Labor Robert Reich portrays millennial America as a nation of strivers who are shifting their goals in ways that affect every business, as well as the strivers themselves.

Keep or Sell Your Business
By Mike Cohn
Dearborn, Chicago, 2001
Mike Cohn is a family business consultant who specializes in helping family business owners manage the transition between generations. His book is a streetwise distillation of many years and many deals, and the problems and solutions he has encountered.

Rebels Against the Future: The Luddites and Their War on the Industrial Revolution: Lessons for the Computer Age
By Kirkpatrick Sale
Perseus Publishing, Cambridge, Mass., 1996
Kirkpatrick Sale's account of Luddism, a rebellion by nineteenth-century factory workers against the use of textile manufacturing equipment, makes illuminating reading for anyone who feels put upon by technology's intrusions in our modern world.

Winning Decisions: Getting It Right the First Time
By J. Edward Russo and Paul J. H. Schoemaker
Doubleday Currency, New York, 2001

The authors describe a four-step process—Framing, Gathering Intelligence, Coming to Conclusions, and Learning from Experience—that can be used to make decisions in business and other spheres. It's an orderly approach to decision making that avoids being too cumbersome to use in real life.

Periodicals

Telephone numbers for the following business periodicals start with country codes in parentheses when the publications are located outside the United States. Phone numbers are for subscription services only. Check the publication web sites to find out if there is a toll-free or local telephone number you can call.

BusinessWeek
800-635-1200
www.businessweek.com
BusinessWeek's comprehensive and authoritative weekly coverage of news and trends about the world of business is mainly intended for senior executives of big companies in North America. But it does have a section devoted to small business concerns, as well as international editions covering major regions of the world.

The Economist
(44) 20 7830 7000
www.economist.com
The Economist is probably the best-written business periodical. Its worldly viewpoint and often wry tone on topics from finance to theater make it one of the favorites as well. Although its coverage focuses on large multinationals, the London-based weekly also reports on trends and news of interest to entrepreneurs.

Entrepreneur
800-274-6229
www.entrepreneur.com

Since 1977 *Entrepreneur* has provided monthly news, trends, and techniques for small business owners and managers. The magazine is aimed at owners of existing businesses, but there's plenty here for start-ups as well.

Far Eastern Economic Review
(36) 852 2508 4338
www.feer.com
Asia's leading business magazine is published every week in Hong Kong and focuses its coverage on Southeast Asia and China.

Fast Company
800-542-6029
www.fastcompany.com
Fast Company was launched during the mid–1990s to help business owners cope with the revolution wrought by the internet. Readers run the gamut from entrepreneurs to corporate executives. Advice tends toward the inspirational.

Financial Times
800-628-8088 (US and Americas)
44 (0)20 7775 6248 (UK and Europe)
www.ft.com
The London-based daily *Financial Times* employs journalists in more than fifty countries to report on business and other news.

Forbes
800-888-9896
www.forbes.com
If *The Economist* is the best-written business periodical, *Forbes* is probably the most uncompromising. Its no-holds-barred coverage of business includes regular features about and for entrepreneurs and small business owners.

Fortune Small Business
800-777-1444
www.fsb.com

FSB is a small business clone of *Fortune* published ten times per year with the same thoughtful approach to entrepreneurs' problems that its big sister pays to the fabled 500.

Harvard Business Review
800-274-3214
www.hbsp.harvard.edu
If you want to read what the top minds in business are thinking, the *Harvard Business Review* is the place to go. Like most business publications, its target audience is the senior executive of a large corporation, but many of the ideas and practices it discusses eventually trickle down to lifestyle businesses.

Inc.
800-234-0999
www.inc.com
Inc. publishes eighteen times a year with practical, down-to-earth articles about strategies for achieving success and avoiding failure as a small business owner and manager.

Wall Street Journal
800-568-7625
www.wsj.com
As the business world's journal of record, the *Wall Street Journal* covers every aspect of commerce five days a week in its print edition and twenty-four hours a day via its on-line publication. Special columns cover small business, work and family, personal technology, and other topics relevant to lifestyle entrepreneurs in the paper's uniquely authoritative voice.

On-line Resources

BizStats

www.bizstats.com

BizStats offers a vast array of no-charge analytical information for small business owners. You can quickly and easily find out such information as typical profit margins for small businesses in your field, highest failure rates for different types of businesses, and much more.

EntreWorld

www.entreworld.org

EntreWorld is an excellent resource sponsored by the nonprofit Kauffman Center for Entrepreneurial Leadership. Its site contains hundreds of articles, databases, tools, event listings, audio files, and other handy and authoritative aids for entrepreneurs.

Russian SME Resource Centre

http://baltic.rcsme.ru

The Russian SME Resource Centre provides information and resource materials on small business development relevant to Russia and Eastern Europe.

Small Business Success

www.smallbizpartners.com/success/

Small Business Success is a little different from most business magazines in that it's published by a group of major corporations in conjunction with the U.S. government's Small Business Administration. It offers clear, practical, down-to-earth tips for business owners on every aspect of running a small business.

StartupJournal.com

www.startupjournal.com

StartupJournal is the *Wall Street Journal*'s on-line center for entrepreneurs. It contains news and articles including pieces written by freelancers and staff reporters for the *Wall Street Journal* and *Inc.* magazine, as well as databases of franchises and businesses for sale, tools for creating a business plan, and other resources.

UPSIDE Magazine
(888) 998-7743
www.upside.com
UPSIDE's coverage includes businesses, people, trends, and strategies in information technology for companies of all sizes and stages of growth.

U.S. Business Advisor
www.business.gov
The U.S. Business Advisor was created by the National Partnership for Reinventing Government and the Small Business Administration to help business owners get information from and about the more than sixty federal organizations that regulate or aid businesses in some way. Among other things, there are detailed step-by-step guides to starting, funding, and running a business.

Organizations

International Council for Small Business
www.icsb.org
The ICSB, based in St. Louis, Missouri, at St. Louis University, is an umbrella group for small-business organizations and professionals in more than sixty countries. It hosts seminars, sponsors research, and disseminates new information on small business management and entrepreneurial development.

National Federation for Independent Business
www.nfib.org
The NFIB is a Washington, D.C.–based U.S. trade group for small businesses. It conducts research and lobbies for legislation important to small businesses and entrepreneurs.

Organization for Economic Cooperation and Development
www.oecd.com
The Geneva, Switzerland–based OECD is made up of thirty countries and has active relationships with about seventy other countries. It is highly regarded for its on-line databases of statistics and publications on trade, education, science, economics, and related issues.

Small Business Service
www.businesslink.org
This agency of the Department of Trade and Industry is aimed at assisting small- and medium-sized enterprises in the United Kingdom. Its on-line Business Link portal provides well-selected information and advice useful for small business owners everywhere.

Index